JAMAICA TRAVEL GUIDE 2024 EDITION

All rights reserved. No part of this publication may be reproduced, distributed, or transmitted in any form or by any means, including photocopying, recording or other electronic or mechanical methods, without the prior written permission of the publisher, except in the case of brief quotation embodied in critical reviews and certain other noncommercial uses permitted by copyright law.

Copyright by Tina Dawson

TABLE OF CONTENTS

INTRODUCTION

Welcome to Jamaica

Quick Facts about Jamaica

SECTION 1: PLANNING YOUR TRIP

Best Time to Visit

Visa and Entry Requirements

Currency and Money Matters

Health and Safety Information

SECTION 2: GETTING THERE

Air Travel

Cruise Options

SECTION 3: DESTINATIONS

Kingston

- *Historical Sites*

- *Dining and Nightlife*

- *Resorts and Hotels*

- *Budget-Friendly Options*

- *Shopping*

- *Beaches and Water Activities*

Montego Bay

- *Historical Sites*

- *Dining and Nightlife*

- *Resorts and Hotels*

- *Budget-Friendly Options*

- *Shopping*

- *Beaches and Water Activities*

Ocho Rios

- Historical Sites

- Dining and Nightlife

- Resorts and Hotels

- Budget-Friendly Options

- Shopping

- Beaches and Water Activities

SECTION 4: ACTIVITIES AND EXCURSIONS

Hiking and Nature Trails

Reggae Music and Dance

Local Festivals and Events

SECTION 5: CUISINE

Jamaican Dishes to Try

Street Food

Fine Dining Experiences

Beverage Specialties

PRACTICAL INFORMATION

Common phrases in Jamaica

INTRODUCTION

Welcome to Jamaica

Jamaica, the jewel of the Caribbean, extends a warm and vibrant welcome to all who venture onto its shores. Nestled in the heart of the Caribbean Sea, this island nation captivates visitors with its rich cultural tapestry, breathtaking landscapes, and the infectious rhythm of reggae music that seems to echo through the air. As you step into this tropical paradise, you are greeted not just by the sun-kissed beaches and lush mountains but also by the genuine smiles of the Jamaican people, known for their hospitality and friendliness.

The allure of Jamaica lies not only In its stunning natural beauty but also in its diverse and fascinating history. The roots of the nation stretch back to the indigenous Taino people and the arrival of Christopher Columbus in 1494. Over the centuries, Jamaica has seen the ebb and flow of colonial powers, including Spanish and British influences, shaping its unique identity. Today, remnants of this history can be explored in the historical sites, museums, and cultural landmarks that dot the island.

The heartbeat of Jamaica is undoubtedly its music. Reggae, born on these very shores, has transcended borders and become a symbol of the island's spirit. From the lively beats of Bob Marley to the contemporary sounds of emerging artists, the music of Jamaica serves as a powerful expression of its people's resilience, joy, and determination. Visitors can immerse themselves in this musical heritage, attending concerts, exploring the Bob Marley Museum in Kingston, or simply swaying to the tunes at a local beachside bar.

For those seeking tranquility, Jamaica offers a haven of natural wonders. The Blue Mountains, draped in emerald-green foliage, provide a sanctuary for hikers and nature enthusiasts. The cascading waters of Dunn's River Falls invite adventure seekers to climb its terraced limestone steps, while the serene waters of the Martha Brae River beckon visitors for a leisurely bamboo raft ride. Each corner of the island reveals a new facet of its natural beauty, from the hidden coves of Treasure Beach to the bustling markets of Ocho Rios.

Culinary enthusiasts will find their palates delighted by the flavors of Jamaican cuisine. Jerk chicken, patties, and the aromatic rice and peas are just a taste of the island's culinary offerings. The fusion of African, Spanish, and indigenous influences has created a vibrant food culture that reflects the diversity of Jamaica itself. Local markets and roadside stalls provide an authentic experience, allowing visitors to savor the island's gastronomic delights while engaging with the friendly vendors.

Jamaica's warmth extends beyond its climate to the hearts of its people. Locals, proud of their heritage, are eager to share the best of Jamaica with visitors. Whether engaging in a friendly chat with a street vendor, joining a spontaneous dance party, or participating in a lively domino game, visitors quickly discover the true essence of Jamaican hospitality. The concept of "One Love" is not just a slogan but a way of life, embodying the unity and acceptance that define the Jamaican spirit.

As the sun sets over the Caribbean horizon, casting a warm glow on the sandy beaches, visitors may find themselves reflecting on the magic of Jamaica. It's a place where time seems to slow down, allowing for a genuine connection with the surroundings and the people. Whether you seek adventure, relaxation, or a cultural awakening, Jamaica welcomes you with open arms, inviting you to experience the rhythm, the flavor, and the soul of this enchanting island nation. Welcome to Jamaica – a destination where every moment is infused with the spirit of the Caribbean, creating memories that will linger long after your departure.

Quick Facts about Jamaica

Jamaica's geographical location places it in the Greater Antilles, part of the Caribbean archipelago. It is the third-largest island in the region, measuring approximately 4,240 square miles. Surrounded by azure waters, Jamaica boasts a diverse topography, encompassing lush mountains, fertile plains, and pristine beaches.

The capital and largest city, Kingston, serves as the cultural and economic hub of Jamaica. It is a vibrant metropolis where visitors can experience the dynamic fusion of modern urban life and traditional Jamaican culture. Other major cities include Montego Bay, Ocho Rios, and Negril, each offering its own unique charm and attractions.

Jamaica's tropical climate is characterized by warm temperatures throughout the year. The average temperature ranges from 77°F to 88°F (25°C to 31°C), providing an ideal environment for a variety of outdoor activities. The island experiences a wet season from May to October, with the possibility of occasional hurricanes due to its location in the hurricane belt.

Home to a population of over 2.9 million people, Jamaica's demographics reflect a rich tapestry of ethnicities and cultures. The majority of the population is of African descent, with smaller communities of Afro-European, East Indian, and Chinese heritage. This cultural diversity is evident in the island's music, cuisine, and traditions.

The official language of Jamaica is English, a legacy of its colonial history. However, the Jamaican Patois, a creole language with West African influences, is widely spoken and adds a distinctive flavor to local communication. Visitors may find the use of Patois charming and engaging, reflecting the island's cultural authenticity.

Jamaica gained its independence from British rule on August 6, 1962, and since then, it has evolved into a proud and sovereign nation. The Jamaican flag, with its bold green, yellow, and black colors, symbolizes the nation's natural wealth, sunshine, and the strength and creativity of its people.

Reggae music, synonymous with Jamaica, has made an indelible mark on global culture. The genre originated in the 1960s, with legendary artists like Bob Marley and Peter Tosh bringing international recognition to Jamaican music. Reggae's rhythmic beats and socially conscious lyrics continue to resonate worldwide, embodying the spirit of the island.

Jamaica's economy is diverse, with key sectors including tourism, agriculture, mining, and manufacturing. The tourism industry plays a pivotal role in driving economic growth, attracting millions of visitors annually. From the bustling streets of Kingston to the serene beaches of

Negril, Jamaica offers a spectrum of experiences for travelers seeking relaxation, adventure, and cultural immersion.

The natural beauty of Jamaica is showcased in its numerous attractions, including the Blue Mountains, Dunn's River Falls, and the Seven Mile Beach. The Blue Mountains, with their mist-shrouded peaks, are a haven for hikers and nature enthusiasts. Dunn's River Falls, a cascading waterfall near Ocho Rios, invites visitors to climb its terraced steps, providing a thrilling and refreshing experience.

The coastal town of Negril is renowned for its stunning Seven Mile Beach, where powdery white sand meets crystal-clear waters. This idyllic stretch is a paradise for sun-seekers and water sports enthusiasts alike. The vibrant coral reefs surrounding the island offer world-class snorkeling and diving opportunities, allowing visitors to explore the underwater wonders of the Caribbean Sea.

Jamaica's culinary scene is a delectable fusion of flavors influenced by African, Indian, Spanish, and British cuisines. Jerk chicken and pork, seasoned with a blend of spices and slow-cooked over pimento wood, are iconic Jamaican dishes. Ackee and saltfish, the national dish, combines the indigenous ackee fruit with salted cod, creating a savory and satisfying meal.

The island's street food culture is vibrant, with local vendors offering specialties such as patties, bammy, and festivals. Patties, flaky pastry filled with spiced meat or vegetables, are a popular snack enjoyed by locals and visitors alike. Bammy, a flatbread made from cassava, and festivals, sweet fried dough, add a delightful variety to Jamaica's culinary landscape.

Jamaica's rich cultural heritage is celebrated through its festivals and events. The annual Carnival, held in Kingston and Montego Bay, is a colorful extravaganza featuring vibrant parades, lively music, and elaborate costumes. The Maroon Festival, honoring the descendants of runaway slaves known as the Maroons, showcases traditional dance, music, and culinary traditions.

Sports hold a special place in Jamaican culture, with athletics being a source of national pride. Jamaica's athletes, particularly in track and field, have achieved global recognition, with legends like Usain Bolt setting world records and inspiring future generations. Cricket is another beloved sport, with passionate local and international competitions held throughout the year.

The warm and welcoming spirit of the Jamaican people, often referred to as "Jamaican hospitality," contributes to the island's allure. Visitors are greeted with open arms, and the locals are known for their friendliness and willingness to share the beauty of their culture. This sense of community extends to the vibrant markets, where artisans showcase their crafts, and street vendors offer a taste of local life.

Jamaica's commitment to sustainable tourism is evident in its efforts to preserve its natural resources and support local communities. Eco-friendly initiatives, such as marine conservation projects and sustainable agriculture practices, contribute to the long-term well-being of the island. Travelers are encouraged to engage in responsible tourism, respecting the environment and embracing the local culture with mindfulness.

Jamaica is a destination that captivates the senses and leaves an indelible mark on those who experience its beauty. From the rhythmic beats of reggae music to the tantalizing flavors of its cuisine, Jamaica offers a rich tapestry of experiences for travelers seeking adventure, relaxation, and cultural immersion. As you explore the vibrant cities, lush landscapes, and pristine beaches, you'll discover why Jamaica is not just an island but a soul-stirring journey that lingers in the heart and memory.

SECTION 1: PLANNING YOUR TRIP

Best Time to Visit

The high tourist season in Jamaica typically occurs from mid-December to mid-January, coinciding with the Christmas and New Year holidays. During this time, the weather is at its peak, characterized by warm temperatures, clear skies, and minimal rainfall. The island comes alive with festivities, making it an ideal period for those seeking a lively atmosphere and engaging in celebratory events.

Following the high season, the shoulder seasons of late January to early February and late November to early December present an appealing compromise. The weather remains pleasant, and visitors can enjoy a less crowded experience compared to the peak months. Accommodation and travel expenses may also be more budget-friendly during these periods.

For travelers looking to avoid the crowds and take advantage of discounted rates, the low season, spanning from mid-April to early December, is worth considering. However, it's crucial to note that this period coincides with the hurricane season in the Caribbean. While Jamaica is not as frequently affected by hurricanes as some other islands, there is still a risk of tropical storms and heavy rainfall. Visitors should monitor weather forecasts and consider travel insurance during these months.

If your primary focus is outdoor activities and exploring Jamaica's natural beauty, the dry season from December to mid-December is an excellent choice. During this time, rainfall is minimal, and the landscape is lush and vibrant. It's an ideal period for hiking, water sports, and enjoying the island's diverse flora and fauna.

Conversely, if you are a fan of reggae music and cultural events, planning your visit around Jamaica's festival season may be more appealing. The Reggae Sumfest, held in Montego Bay in July, is one of the largest reggae music festivals in the world, drawing international artists and music enthusiasts.

Determining the best time to visit Jamaica depends on your preferences and priorities. Whether you seek a festive atmosphere, budget-friendly options, or specific weather conditions for outdoor activities, Jamaica offers a variety of experiences year-round. Understanding the distinct characteristics of each season will enable you to make an informed decision and ensure a memorable and enjoyable stay on this captivating Caribbean island.

Visa and Entry Requirements

Jamaica maintains a welcoming approach to tourism, but like any international destination, certain regulations must be adhered to. The country's visa and entry requirements are designed to facilitate smooth entry for visitors while ensuring the safety and security of both tourists and locals.

Visa Requirements:

Tourist Visas:

Jamaica has a relatively straightforward visa policy, and many nationalities can enter the country for tourism purposes without obtaining a visa in advance. Travelers from visa-exempt countries are granted entry for a specified period upon arrival. It's crucial to check the official Jamaican government website or contact the nearest Jamaican embassy or consulate to confirm the current visa requirements for your specific nationality.

Visa-Exempt Countries:

As of the last update, citizens of several countries, including the United States, Canada, the United Kingdom, and many European nations, do not require a visa for stays of up to a certain number of days. The duration of permitted stays varies depending on the visitor's nationality. Travelers must possess a passport valid for at least six months beyond their intended departure date.

Visa on Arrival:

For citizens of countries not covered by the visa-exempt policy, Jamaica offers a visa-on-arrival option. This allows eligible travelers to obtain a visa upon reaching the Jamaican port of entry.

The visa on arrival is typically granted for short stays, and specific requirements, such as proof of return or onward travel, may apply.

Entry Requirements:

Passport:

A valid passport is a fundamental requirement for entry into Jamaica. It must be valid for at least six months beyond the intended departure date. Visitors are urged to check their passport's expiration date well in advance of their travel dates to avoid any complications.

Return or Onward Ticket:

To enter Jamaica, travelers may be required to provide proof of return or onward travel. This ensures that visitors do not overstay their authorized period and have a clear departure plan.

Immigration Form:

Upon arrival in Jamaica, visitors are usually required to complete an immigration form. This form collects essential information, including the purpose of the visit, accommodation details, and contact information. It is advisable to complete this form accurately and retain the provided copy for departure procedures.

Yellow Fever Vaccination:

Jamaica may require travelers arriving from certain countries with a risk of yellow fever transmission to present a valid yellow fever vaccination certificate. This requirement aims to prevent the introduction of the virus into the country.

Compliance and Extensions:

Overstaying:

It is crucial for visitors to adhere to the authorized duration of their stay. Overstaying without proper authorization can result in fines, deportation, or other legal consequences. If unforeseen circumstances arise, it's advisable to contact local immigration authorities to discuss possible extensions before the authorized period expires.

Visa Extensions:

For travelers who wish to extend their stay beyond the initially granted period, visa extensions may be available. However, extension policies can vary, and it's recommended to inquire at the nearest immigration office or contact relevant authorities for guidance.

Understanding and complying with Jamaica's visa and entry requirements is essential for a smooth and enjoyable visit. By ensuring that all necessary documents are in order and adhering to the regulations, travelers can focus on exploring the beauty and warmth that Jamaica has to offer. Always check for the latest updates on visa policies and entry requirements, as these can be subject to change. With the right preparation, your Jamaican adventure awaits, promising a blend of relaxation, adventure, and unforgettable experiences.

Jamaica's Currency and Money Matters

Jamaica, a vibrant island nation in the Caribbean, boasts not only stunning landscapes and rich cultural experiences but also a unique monetary system that reflects its history and economic dynamics. Understanding the currency and managing your money effectively is crucial for a smooth and enjoyable trip to this tropical paradise.

The Jamaican Dollar (JMD)

The official currency of Jamaica is the Jamaican Dollar (JMD). Symbolized as "$" or "J$", it is the primary medium of exchange for goods and services. The Bank of Jamaica is the country's central bank responsible for issuing and regulating the Jamaican Dollar. Travelers should familiarize themselves with the current exchange rates to make informed financial decisions during their stay.

Currency Denominations

The Jamaican Dollar comes in various denominations, including coins and banknotes. Coins are available in values of 1, 5, 10, and 25 dollars, while banknotes are issued in denominations of 50, 100, 500, 1,000, and 5,000 dollars. The different denominations make it convenient for transactions of various sizes, from small purchases to larger expenses.

Exchange Rates and Conversion

Before traveling to Jamaica, it is advisable to check the current exchange rates. Currency exchange services are available at airports, banks, and authorized currency exchange offices across the country. Many hotels and resorts also offer currency exchange services, but it's essential to be aware of the potential fees and less favorable rates in such establishments.

Credit Cards and ATMs

Credit cards, particularly Visa and Mastercard, are widely accepted in urban areas, major tourist destinations, and established businesses. However, it's prudent to carry some cash for transactions in more remote or local areas where card acceptance may be limited. Automated Teller Machines (ATMs) are readily available in cities and towns, providing a convenient way to withdraw Jamaican Dollars. Be mindful of transaction fees and currency conversion charges associated with using ATMs.

Traveler's Checks

While traveler's checks were once a popular option for secure travel funds, their usage has declined in recent years. Many businesses in Jamaica may not readily accept traveler's checks, and the process of cashing them can be time-consuming. It's advisable to rely on a combination of cash and credit/debit cards for greater convenience.

Tipping Culture

Tipping is a common practice in Jamaica, and it is appreciated for services such as dining, tour guides, and hotel staff. While some restaurants may include a service charge, it's customary to leave an additional tip for exceptional service. Tipping in local currency is preferred, so it's helpful to have smaller denominations of Jamaican Dollars on hand.

Budgeting and Expenses

Creating a realistic budget for your Jamaican adventure is crucial for a stress-free vacation. Consider factors such as accommodation, meals, transportation, activities, and souvenirs when planning your expenses. Researching average costs in advance and accounting for unexpected expenses ensures that you can fully enjoy your time without financial concerns.

Currency and Cultural Sensitivity

Respect for the local currency is a reflection of cultural sensitivity. While the Jamaican Dollar may have a different value compared to your home currency, it's essential to approach financial transactions with respect and understanding. Familiarizing yourself with Jamaican currency and its cultural significance enhances your overall travel experience.

Navigating Jamaica's currency and money matters adds a practical dimension to your travel preparations. By being aware of the Jamaican Dollar denominations, exchange rates, and preferred payment methods, you set the stage for a seamless and enjoyable journey. Embrace the vibrant culture, savor the local cuisine, and explore the island's wonders with the confidence that comes from understanding the nuances of currency and money matters in Jamaica.

Health and Safety Information in Jamaica

Jamaica, a picturesque island known for its vibrant culture, lush landscapes, and warm hospitality, is a popular destination for travelers seeking sun, sand, and adventure. To ensure a safe and enjoyable visit, it's crucial to be aware of health and safety considerations that may impact your stay.

Healthcare Facilities

Jamaica boasts modern healthcare facilities, particularly in major urban areas such as Kingston and Montego Bay. Hospitals and medical centers offer a range of services, from routine check-ups to emergency care. It is advisable to have travel insurance that covers medical expenses, as this can provide financial security in case of unexpected health issues.

Vaccinations and Health Precautions

Before traveling to Jamaica, it is essential to check the recommended and required vaccinations. Common vaccinations include hepatitis A and B, typhoid, and routine shots. Mosquito-borne illnesses, such as dengue fever and Zika virus, are present in some regions, so travelers should use insect repellent and take necessary precautions to avoid mosquito bites.

Food and Water Safety

While Jamaican cuisine is a delight for the senses, it's crucial to exercise caution to prevent foodborne illnesses. Stick to reputable restaurants and avoid consuming raw or undercooked seafood. Drink bottled or purified water and be wary of ice in drinks, especially in more rural areas.

Sun Safety

Jamaica's tropical climate means abundant sunshine, making sunscreen an essential item for your packing list. Protect yourself from harmful UV rays by applying sunscreen regularly, wearing hats and sunglasses, and seeking shade during peak sun hours.

Beach Safety

Jamaica's stunning beaches are a major attraction, but it's important to be mindful of safety guidelines. Pay attention to local beach flags indicating water conditions, and adhere to lifeguard instructions. While the clear waters are inviting, it's crucial to be aware of potential dangers such as strong currents.

Road Safety

If you plan to explore the island by car, familiarize yourself with Jamaican road rules and conditions. Drive on the left side of the road, and exercise caution on winding or rural routes. Seatbelts are mandatory, and it's advisable to avoid driving at night, especially in less populated areas.

Local Wildlife

Jamaica is home to diverse wildlife, including some species that may pose risks to humans. While encounters with dangerous animals are rare, it's essential to be cautious in natural habitats. Avoid disturbing wildlife, and if hiking or exploring rural areas, be aware of your surroundings.

Cultural Sensitivity

Respect for local customs and traditions is integral to a positive travel experience. Jamaican culture is warm and welcoming, but it's important to be mindful of local etiquette. Dress modestly in religious or rural areas, and ask for permission before photographing people.

Emergency Contacts

In case of emergencies, it's crucial to know the local emergency contact numbers. The general emergency number is 119, and medical assistance can be obtained by dialing 110. Save these numbers in your phone and, if possible, have a list of local contacts or your country's embassy.

Jamaica's allure extends beyond its stunning landscapes to the warmth of its people and the richness of its culture. By prioritizing health and safety considerations, you can fully immerse yourself in the beauty of this Caribbean gem. Whether you're exploring the vibrant cities or relaxing on the sun-kissed beaches, a mindful approach to health and safety ensures a memorable and worry-free Jamaican experience.

SECTION 2: GETTING THERE

Navigating the Skies: A Comprehensive Guide to Airlines Flying to Jamaica

Jamaica, with its vibrant culture, stunning landscapes, and warm hospitality, is a popular destination for travelers worldwide. As you plan your journey to this Caribbean paradise, understanding the options for airlines that connect you to Jamaica is crucial. In this guide, we will delve into the various airlines that serve Jamaica, exploring their routes, services, and unique features that contribute to a seamless travel experience.

1. Major International Airlines

1.1 American Airlines

Routes: American Airlines offers extensive services to Jamaica from major U.S. cities, including Miami, New York, and Dallas.

Services: Explore the perks of flying with American Airlines, such as in-flight entertainment, comfortable seating options, and diverse dining choices.

1.2 Delta Air Lines

Routes: Delta operates flights to Jamaica from Atlanta, New York, and other key hubs.

Services: Learn about Delta's commitment to customer satisfaction, with features like Wi-Fi, complimentary snacks, and Delta Sky Club access.

1.3 United Airlines

Routes: United connects travelers to Jamaica from Chicago, Houston, and Newark.

Services: Discover the in-flight amenities, baggage policies, and loyalty programs that make United a preferred choice.

2. Caribbean Airlines

2.1 Overview

Hub: Trinidad and Tobago

Routes: Delve into Caribbean Airlines' network, connecting Jamaica to other Caribbean destinations and beyond.

Services: Explore the regional flavor of Caribbean Airlines, including local cuisine and a vibrant in-flight atmosphere.

3. Jamaican-Based Airlines

3.1 Air Jamaica (Now Caribbean Airlines)

History: Reflect on the legacy of Air Jamaica and its integration into Caribbean Airlines.

Routes: Understand how the merger has expanded the reach and services available to travelers.

3.2 Fly Jamaica Airways

Overview: Learn about this Jamaican carrier, its routes, and its commitment to providing a unique travel experience.

Services: Explore the in-flight services and entertainment options that set Fly Jamaica Airways apart.

4. Low-Cost Carriers

4.1 Southwest Airlines

Routes: Southwest's entry into the Jamaican market has brought affordable options from various U.S. cities.

Services: Uncover the budget-friendly services and policies that make Southwest an attractive choice for budget-conscious travelers.

4.2 Spirit Airlines

Routes: Spirit Airlines provides a range of options for travelers seeking economical flights to Jamaica.

Services: Despite its low-cost model, discover how Spirit ensures a comfortable journey with various add-on services.

5. Connecting Flights and Hubs

5.1 Miami International Airport

Overview: Explore the significance of Miami as a major hub for flights to Jamaica and the convenience of connecting flights.

5.2 Hartsfield-Jackson Atlanta International Airport

Connecting Options: Understand the advantages of connecting through Atlanta, a key hub for multiple airlines.

6. Tips for Booking and Traveling

6.1 Best Times to Book

Seasonal Trends: Discover the optimal times to secure affordable tickets to Jamaica.

6.2 Traveling with Airlines to Jamaica

Baggage Policies: Understand the baggage allowances, restrictions, and tips for hassle-free travel.

As you embark on your journey to Jamaica, the selection of the right airline plays a pivotal role in shaping your travel experience. Whether you prioritize luxury, affordability, or a regional touch, the diverse array of airlines servicing Jamaica ensures that there's an option for every traveler. Stay informed, plan wisely, and get ready to soar into the enchanting skies on your way to the heart of the Caribbean.

American Airlines: Soaring to Jamaica's Tropical Rhythms

As the sun dips below the horizon, casting a warm glow on the azure waters of the Caribbean, Jamaica beckons travelers from around the world. For those seeking a seamless journey to this island paradise, American Airlines stands as a stalwart companion, offering extensive routes, world-class services, and a commitment to delivering passengers to their Jamaican getaway with style and efficiency.

The American Airlines Experience

The Network

American Airlines boasts an expansive network connecting the United States to various destinations across the globe. When it comes to Jamaica, American Airlines serves as a vital link, providing numerous options for travelers to reach the island. Key departure points include major cities such as Miami, New York, and Dallas.

Miami Gateway

Miami, with its vibrant international airport, serves as a crucial gateway for American Airlines' flights to Jamaica. The strategic location of Miami facilitates convenient connections, making it a preferred choice for travelers from different parts of the United States.

New York Connection

New York, a city that never sleeps, serves as another prominent departure point for American Airlines' flights to Jamaica. Whether you're embarking on your Jamaican adventure from JFK International Airport or Newark Liberty International Airport, American Airlines offers a range of options to suit your travel plans.

Dallas Departures

For those in the southwestern United States, Dallas/Fort Worth International Airport is a key hub for American Airlines. Travelers can catch flights from Dallas to Jamaica, experiencing the airline's renowned services and amenities throughout their journey.

In-Flight Comforts

American Airlines prioritizes passenger comfort, ensuring that the journey to Jamaica is as enjoyable as the destination itself. With a fleet of modern aircraft, travelers can expect spacious cabins, ergonomic seating, and a range of in-flight entertainment options.

Entertainment Options

Long flights become a breeze with American Airlines' diverse entertainment offerings. From the latest blockbuster movies to TV shows and music, there's something for every passenger's taste. The airline's in-flight entertainment system ensures that the journey is not just a means of transportation but a part of the overall travel experience.

Dining at Altitude

American Airlines elevates the dining experience at 30,000 feet. Passengers traveling to Jamaica can savor a variety of culinary delights, from carefully curated meals to snacks and beverages. The airline's commitment to providing quality dining options reflects its dedication to offering a premium travel experience.

Connectivity and Technology

In today's interconnected world, staying connected during travel is paramount. American Airlines understands this need and provides reliable in-flight Wi-Fi, allowing passengers to stay in touch with loved ones, work remotely, or simply browse the internet while cruising towards the Jamaican shores.

Loyalty Programs

Frequent flyers with American Airlines enjoy the benefits of the AAdvantage loyalty program. As passengers accrue miles, they unlock a range of privileges, including priority boarding, access to exclusive lounges, and the flexibility to use miles for future travel.

Navigating the Booking Process

Booking Flexibility

American Airlines recognizes the diverse needs of travelers, and its booking process reflects this understanding. Whether you're a solo adventurer, a couple seeking a romantic retreat, or a family planning a tropical vacation, American Airlines offers a variety of fare classes and booking options to cater to different preferences and budgets.

Seasonal Considerations

Understanding the seasonal trends can be pivotal when planning a trip to Jamaica. American Airlines provides insights into the best times to book flights, allowing travelers to take advantage of competitive fares and secure their tickets for an optimal Jamaican experience.

Travel Tips and Considerations

Baggage Policies

Navigating baggage policies can be a concern for travelers, but American Airlines simplifies the process with transparent guidelines. Passengers heading to Jamaica can familiarize themselves with the airline's baggage allowances, restrictions, and tips for hassle-free travel.

Health and Safety Measures

In the ever-evolving landscape of global travel, health and safety have become paramount concerns. American Airlines has implemented robust measures to ensure the well-being of passengers, including enhanced cleaning protocols, air filtration systems, and adherence to public health guidelines.

The Jamaican Connection: Beyond the Skies

Beyond the logistics of flying, American Airlines recognizes the cultural significance of Jamaica. The airline strives to create a sense of anticipation and connection to the destination, infusing the journey with the spirit of the Caribbean. Whether it's the warm hospitality of the cabin crew or the curated in-flight experiences, American Airlines seeks to set the tone for the Jamaican adventure from the moment passengers step onboard.

In the tapestry of airlines connecting the world, American Airlines emerges as a vibrant thread weaving through the skies to Jamaica. As travelers embark on this Caribbean escapade, American Airlines stands as a reliable partner, offering not just transportation but an experience. From the bustling airports of the United States to the tropical allure of Jamaica, American Airlines ensures that the journey is as memorable as the destination. So, fasten your seatbelts, relax in the comfort of your seat, and let American Airlines transport you to the rhythmic shores of Jamaica.

Delta Air Lines: Soaring to the Heart of the Caribbean

Delta Air Lines, a behemoth in the aviation industry, stands as a key player in connecting global travelers to diverse destinations, including the sun-kissed shores of Jamaica. As we delve into the intricacies of Delta's services to this Caribbean paradise, it becomes apparent that the airline is not merely a means of transportation but a facilitator of seamless journeys, creating experiences that linger in the minds of passengers.

Delta's Global Network

Delta Air Lines boasts an extensive global network, with a significant presence in North America, Europe, Asia, and beyond. This robust network serves as the backbone for its flights to Jamaica, providing travelers with numerous options to reach this tropical haven.

U.S. Hubs

Delta operates flights to Jamaica from several major U.S. hubs, with Atlanta being a primary gateway. As one of the busiest airports globally, Hartsfield-Jackson Atlanta International Airport serves as a crucial hub for connecting flights to Jamaica and various other destinations.

New York and Beyond

New York's John F. Kennedy International Airport is another pivotal departure point for Delta's flights to Jamaica. The airline connects the Big Apple to the vibrant culture and turquoise waters of Jamaica, offering travelers convenience and choice.

The Delta Experience

In-Flight Comfort

Delta is synonymous with comfort, and this extends to its flights to Jamaica. Passengers can expect spacious seating, adjustable headrests, and ample legroom, ensuring a relaxing journey from takeoff to touchdown. Delta's commitment to passenger well-being is evident in its ergonomically designed seats, which cater to the needs of both business and leisure travelers.

Entertainment at 30,000 Feet

One of the hallmarks of Delta's service is its in-flight entertainment. Whether you're flying short-haul or embarking on a transatlantic journey to Jamaica, Delta ensures that boredom is never on the itinerary. The airline's state-of-the-art entertainment system offers a vast selection of movies, TV shows, music, and games, catering to a diverse range of tastes.

Culinary Delights

Delta understands that the journey itself is an integral part of the travel experience. As passengers make their way to Jamaica, they can savor a culinary journey with Delta's onboard dining options. From delectable snacks to gourmet meals, the airline strives to provide a taste of luxury at 30,000 feet.

Delta Sky Club

For those seeking an elevated pre-flight or layover experience, Delta Sky Club lounges are a haven of tranquility. With complimentary snacks, beverages, and Wi-Fi, these lounges offer an escape from the hustle and bustle of the airport, allowing travelers to unwind before their journey to Jamaica.

Delta's Commitment to Safety

Safety is paramount in aviation, and Delta Air Lines has a stellar track record in this regard. The airline invests in cutting-edge technology, rigorous training programs, and a meticulous approach to maintenance to ensure the well-being of its passengers. Travelers on Delta's flights to Jamaica can embark on their adventures with the confidence that their safety is the airline's top priority.

SkyMiles: Elevating the Travel Experience

Delta's SkyMiles loyalty program is a testament to the airline's commitment to rewarding its frequent flyers. Passengers on Delta's flights to Jamaica can accrue miles that open the door to a world of benefits, including seat upgrades, priority boarding, and access to exclusive lounges. SkyMiles members experience travel not just as a journey but as a continuous exploration, with each flight bringing them closer to exciting perks and privileges.

Environmental Stewardship

In an era where environmental concerns are at the forefront, Delta Air Lines is taking strides to minimize its carbon footprint. From investing in fuel-efficient aircraft to implementing sustainable practices, the airline is dedicated to environmental stewardship. Travelers can embark on their journey to Jamaica with the knowledge that Delta is committed to a more sustainable future for aviation.

Delta's Community Engagement

Beyond the confines of the aircraft, Delta Air Lines actively engages with communities, both locally and globally. The airline supports various charitable initiatives, fostering a sense of social responsibility. As passengers journey to Jamaica with Delta, they become part of a larger narrative, contributing to the positive impact the airline strives to create.

In the realm of aviation, Delta Air Lines stands as a paragon of excellence, seamlessly connecting travelers to the enchanting shores of Jamaica. From the moment passengers step on board to the time they disembark, Delta's commitment to comfort, safety, and customer satisfaction is evident. As travelers embark on their journey with Delta, they are not merely flying to a destination; they are experiencing a blend of luxury, efficiency, and a genuine passion for travel. Delta Air Lines doesn't just bridge the gap between departure and arrival—it transforms the act of flying into an integral part of the adventure, leaving indelible memories on the way to the heart of the Caribbean.

United Airlines to Jamaica: A Comprehensive Exploration

United Airlines, one of the major players in the global aviation industry, serves as a vital link between the United States and the Caribbean, including the sun-kissed island of Jamaica. In this detailed exploration, we delve into the various aspects of United Airlines' operations to Jamaica, from its history and routes to the in-flight experience and the unique features that set it apart in the competitive world of air travel.

United Airlines, founded in 1926, has grown to become one of the largest and most influential airlines globally. Over the years, the airline has expanded its network, connecting passengers to destinations across six continents. United's foray into the Caribbean, including Jamaica, is a testament to its commitment to providing comprehensive air travel services.

Routes to Jamaica

United Airlines offers travelers a range of options for reaching the Caribbean gem of Jamaica. Key departure points include major U.S. cities like Chicago, Houston, and Newark. These well-connected hubs serve as gateways for passengers embarking on their journey to the vibrant island.

The Chicago O'Hare International Airport, a major hub for United Airlines, acts as a crucial departure point for flights to Jamaica. Travelers can seamlessly connect through this bustling airport, ensuring a smooth and efficient travel experience.

Houston's George Bush Intercontinental Airport is another strategic hub for United's flights to Jamaica. The airport's extensive connectivity and modern facilities contribute to a convenient and enjoyable journey for passengers en route to the Caribbean.

Newark Liberty International Airport, located in the New York metropolitan area, serves as a vital link for travelers from the northeastern United States seeking direct flights to Jamaica. United's operations from Newark provide a gateway for a diverse range of passengers.

United Airlines is renowned for its commitment to providing a comfortable and enjoyable in-flight experience. Passengers traveling to Jamaica with United can expect a range of amenities designed to enhance their journey.

United offers a diverse selection of in-flight entertainment, including the latest movies, TV shows, music, and more. With personal screens and a variety of content, passengers can tailor their entertainment experience to suit their preferences.

United provides a range of seating options to accommodate the diverse needs of travelers. From Economy to Business and First Class, passengers can choose the level of comfort and services that align with their preferences and budget.

United Airlines is committed to offering a culinary experience that reflects the diversity of its passengers. The airline provides a selection of meals and snacks, including special dietary options, ensuring that every traveler's palate is catered to.

United Airlines operates one of the most popular frequent flyer programs, MileagePlus. Passengers traveling to Jamaica and other destinations with United can accrue miles that can be redeemed for future flights, upgrades, and a range of other benefits. The loyalty program enhances the overall travel experience, incentivizing passengers to choose United repeatedly.

United Airlines places a strong emphasis on customer service, recognizing the pivotal role it plays in shaping the passenger experience. The airline provides multiple channels for customer support, including online assistance, phone support, and in-person service at airports. This commitment to customer satisfaction contributes to United's positive reputation in the aviation industry.

Efficiency in operations and punctuality are crucial factors in the airline industry, and United Airlines strives to excel in both. Passengers flying to Jamaica can expect timely departures and arrivals, contributing to a hassle-free travel experience.

In an era where environmental sustainability is a key concern, United Airlines has taken strides to reduce its carbon footprint. The airline has implemented various initiatives, including investments in fuel-efficient aircraft, sustainable aviation fuels, and waste reduction programs. Travelers to Jamaica with United can appreciate the airline's commitment to environmental responsibility.

United Airlines' operations to Jamaica represent a crucial link between the United States and this enchanting Caribbean destination. With a rich history, a comprehensive network of routes, and a commitment to passenger satisfaction, United stands out as a reliable choice for travelers seeking a seamless journey to Jamaica. Whether you're drawn to the diverse in-flight services, the convenience of well-connected hubs, or the benefits of a robust loyalty program, United Airlines offers a holistic travel experience that extends beyond the skies and into the hearts of those eager to explore the beauty of Jamaica.

Air Jamaica: Soaring to the Heart of the Caribbean

Air travel has long been the conduit that connects the world, turning distant dreams into accessible realities. In the realm of Caribbean destinations, Jamaica stands out as a jewel, beckoning travelers with its lush landscapes, vibrant culture, and warm hospitality. As enthusiasts of the island paradise plan their journeys, one airline has historically played a significant role in ferrying passengers to the rhythmic beats of reggae and the serene beaches of Jamaica – Air Jamaica.

Founded in 1966, Air Jamaica emerged as the national airline of Jamaica, becoming an emblematic carrier that not only facilitated travel but also embodied the spirit and identity of the Caribbean nation. The airline was initially established as a joint venture between the Jamaican government and the British Overseas Airways Corporation (BOAC). Over the years, Air Jamaica became synonymous with the colors of the Jamaican flag, proudly painted on its fleet, and the distinctive "One Love" slogan, which resonated with both locals and visitors alike.

Routes and Destinations

Air Jamaica strategically positioned itself as a key player in the Caribbean aviation landscape, operating flights not only to Jamaica but also to various destinations across the Americas and Europe. The airline's primary hub was Sangster International Airport in Montego Bay, a gateway to Jamaica's enchanting north coast. From this strategic base, Air Jamaica spread its wings, connecting passengers to major cities such as New York, Miami, Toronto, and London.

The carrier's network encompassed a mix of leisure and business destinations, reflecting the multifaceted nature of Jamaica's appeal. Whether it was sun-seeking vacationers drawn to the white sandy beaches of Negril or business travelers navigating the bustling streets of Kingston, Air Jamaica played a vital role in facilitating these journeys, embodying the spirit of Jamaican hospitality from takeoff to touchdown.

The Air Jamaica Experience

Air travel is not merely about reaching a destination; it's also about the journey. Air Jamaica, in its heyday, was known for providing a unique and vibrant in-flight experience that mirrored the island's cultural richness. From the moment passengers stepped aboard, they were enveloped in an atmosphere of warmth and friendliness, with the cabin crew adorned in uniforms reflecting Jamaica's bold and colorful aesthetic.

The airline's commitment to offering a taste of Jamaica extended to its culinary offerings. Passengers were treated to a selection of Jamaican dishes, providing a flavorful introduction to the island's cuisine. The aroma of jerk chicken wafting through the cabin and the taste of coconut-infused delicacies became a hallmark of the Air Jamaica experience, creating lasting memories for those fortunate enough to savor the journey.

As the aviation industry evolved, Air Jamaica faced its share of challenges. Economic pressures, changing market dynamics, and increased competition compelled the airline to adapt. In 2011, Air Jamaica underwent a significant transformation when it was fully acquired by Caribbean Airlines, a Trinidad-based carrier. This marked the end of an era for Air Jamaica as an independent national airline, but it also signaled a new chapter in its history.

The acquisition by Caribbean Airlines brought about changes in the airline's operations, including the integration of routes and services. While the iconic Air Jamaica brand eventually faded from the skies, its legacy lived on in the continued commitment to serving Jamaica and maintaining the island's connectivity with the rest of the world.

For many travelers, Air Jamaica holds a special place in their hearts, not just as a means of transportation but as an embodiment of the Jamaican spirit. The vibrant colors of the aircraft, the lively atmosphere on board, and the friendly faces of the crew left an indelible mark on those who experienced the airline during its peak. Nostalgia for Air Jamaica persists, with enthusiasts reminiscing about the golden age of Caribbean air travel and the role this iconic carrier played in fostering a sense of unity and pride.

While the physical presence of Air Jamaica may no longer grace the runways, its legacy continues to soar through the memories of those who traveled under its wings. The story of Air Jamaica is not just a tale of an airline; it is a narrative woven into the fabric of Jamaica's history and its journey toward becoming a global tourist destination.

As travelers continue to explore the enchanting shores of Jamaica, they can reflect on the times when Air Jamaica was more than a carrier; it was a symbol of the island's warmth, vibrancy, and the promise of an unforgettable journey. In the ever-changing landscape of air travel, Air Jamaica remains an enduring emblem of the magic that happens when a nation's spirit takes flight.

Fly Jamaica Airways: Soaring to the Heart of the Caribbean

Fly Jamaica Airways, a distinctive player in the aviation industry, has carved a niche for itself by providing travelers with a unique and memorable journey to the beautiful island of Jamaica. Established with a commitment to offering quality service and a touch of Jamaican warmth, Fly Jamaica has become synonymous with reliability, comfort, and a genuine Caribbean experience.

Founded in 2011, Fly Jamaica Airways set out to bridge the gap between North America and the Caribbean, with a particular focus on connecting passengers to the enticing shores of Jamaica. The airline's inception was rooted in a vision to not just transport people but to create an atmosphere that reflects the spirit and culture of Jamaica, even at 30,000 feet.

The airline, headquartered in Kingston, Jamaica, embarked on its journey with a fleet that included Boeing 757-200 aircraft, signaling a commitment to modern and reliable aviation technology. As a Jamaican-owned and operated airline, Fly Jamaica quickly gained attention for its distinct approach to air travel, blending efficiency with a warm, hospitable touch that mirrored the island's renowned friendliness.

Fly Jamaica Airways strategically selected its routes to cater to the needs of travelers seeking direct access to Jamaica and other Caribbean destinations. While the airline has undergone changes over the years, its commitment to connecting major North American cities with Jamaica has remained unwavering.

Fly Jamaica initially operated flights between Kingston, Jamaica, and New York City's John F. Kennedy International Airport. This route not only facilitated travel for Jamaican diaspora but also opened doors for international tourists seeking an authentic Jamaican experience. Over time, the airline expanded its route network to include additional destinations, enhancing connectivity and accessibility.

At the core of Fly Jamaica's operational success is its fleet of modern aircraft designed to ensure passenger safety, comfort, and a smooth journey. The Boeing 757-200, known for its reliability and fuel efficiency, has been a cornerstone of Fly Jamaica's fleet. This aircraft choice reflects the airline's commitment to providing a seamless travel experience while maintaining environmental responsibility.

Fly Jamaica has embraced technological advancements in the aviation industry to enhance its operational efficiency. From state-of-the-art avionics to in-flight entertainment systems, the airline has continually invested in technologies that elevate the overall travel experience for its passengers.

One of the hallmarks of Fly Jamaica Airways is its dedication to creating an in-flight experience that mirrors the warmth and vibrancy of Jamaica. From the moment passengers board the aircraft, they are greeted with a friendly and accommodating crew, setting the tone for a journey that goes beyond mere transportation.

In-flight services on Fly Jamaica include a selection of complimentary meals and beverages, ensuring that passengers can savor the flavors of Jamaica even while cruising at high altitudes. The airline takes pride in its culinary offerings, presenting passengers with a taste of authentic Jamaican cuisine, prepared with care to cater to diverse palates.

Entertainment options are thoughtfully curated to provide a mix of cultural insights and contemporary enjoyment. Passengers can immerse themselves in Jamaican music, movies, and documentaries, offering a glimpse into the rich tapestry of the island's heritage.

What sets Fly Jamaica Airways apart is its commitment to infusing the Jamaican culture into every aspect of the travel experience. The airline serves as a flying ambassador, introducing passengers to the essence of Jamaica even before they set foot on the island.

Fly Jamaica's aircraft are adorned with vibrant colors and artwork that celebrate Jamaica's artistic heritage. The airline has collaborated with local artists to create a visual tapestry that reflects the diversity and vibrancy of Jamaican culture. From the exterior livery to the in-flight décor, every detail is a nod to the island's rich heritage.

The crew, trained to embody the warmth and hospitality for which Jamaica is renowned, adds a personal touch to the journey. Passengers often find themselves engaged in friendly conversations with the crew, further enhancing the overall travel experience.

Like any airline, Fly Jamaica Airways has faced its share of challenges. Operational disruptions, economic uncertainties, and the global impact of events such as the COVID-19 pandemic have tested the resilience of the aviation industry as a whole. Fly Jamaica, in navigating these challenges, has demonstrated adaptability and a commitment to passenger well-being.

The airline's response to the pandemic included implementing rigorous safety measures, ensuring that passengers could travel with confidence. Flexible booking options and transparent communication became integral parts of Fly Jamaica's strategy to address the evolving travel landscape.

Fly Jamaica Airways recognizes the importance of giving back to the communities it serves. The airline has been involved in various community engagement initiatives, supporting local causes and contributing to the well-being of Jamaican society.

From educational programs to environmental initiatives, Fly Jamaica aims to be a positive force beyond air travel. The airline understands its role as a corporate citizen and actively seeks opportunities to contribute to the development and sustainability of the communities it connects.

As Fly Jamaica Airways looks to the future, there is a continued commitment to growth and service excellence. The airline envisions expanding its route network to connect more cities with Jamaica, providing travelers with convenient and direct access to the island's wonders.

Fly Jamaica remains attuned to the evolving needs of the modern traveler. Technological advancements, environmental sustainability, and passenger comfort will likely be focal points as the airline positions itself for continued success in the dynamic aviation landscape.

Fly Jamaica Airways has not merely positioned itself as an airline; it has become a symbol of Jamaican pride and hospitality in the skies. With a blend of modern technology, cultural integration, and a commitment to service excellence, Fly Jamaica offers more than a means of transportation—it provides a journey that begins the moment passengers step on board.

For those seeking an authentic Caribbean experience from the moment they embark on their journey, Fly Jamaica Airways stands as a testament to the idea that air travel can be more than a conveyance; it can be a cultural voyage, an introduction to the spirit of a place, and a prelude to

the wonders that await on the shores of Jamaica. Fly Jamaica Airways: where the joy of flying meets the warmth of the Caribbean.

Cruise Options to Jamaica: Navigating the Caribbean Paradise

Jamaica, with its vibrant culture, lush landscapes, and pristine beaches, is a sought-after destination for cruise enthusiasts. Several cruise lines offer exciting itineraries that allow travelers to explore the best of Jamaica. Below, we delve into the cruise options available, detailing departure ports, cruise lines, and the attractions awaiting passengers on this Caribbean island.

1. **Popular Cruise Lines to Jamaica:**

Royal Caribbean International:

Known for its innovative ships, Royal Caribbean offers various itineraries to Jamaica. Ships like Symphony of the Seas and Oasis of the Seas often include stops in ports like Falmouth and Ocho Rios.

Carnival Cruise Line:

Carnival, a favorite for its lively atmosphere, has itineraries that feature stops in Montego Bay. Carnival Breeze and Carnival Conquest are among the ships that may include Jamaica in their Caribbean routes.

Norwegian Cruise Line:

With "freestyle cruising," Norwegian provides flexibility in dining and activities. Ships such as Norwegian Breakaway and Norwegian Escape frequently visit Jamaican ports.

MSC Cruises:

This European cruise line offers a taste of the Caribbean, with some itineraries including stops in Jamaica. MSC Seaside and MSC Meraviglia are popular ships for this route.

2. **Departure Ports:**

Miami, Florida:

Many cruises to Jamaica embark from Miami, known as the "Cruise Capital of the World." This vibrant city serves as a major gateway to the Caribbean.

Fort Lauderdale, Florida:

Another key departure point, Fort Lauderdale's Port Everglades, is a hub for Caribbean cruises, providing convenient access to Jamaica.

Galveston, Texas:

For those seeking a departure port in the southern United States, Galveston offers cruises that make their way to Jamaica.

San Juan, Puerto Rico:

Some itineraries originate from San Juan, providing a unique opportunity to explore the southern Caribbean before reaching Jamaica.

3. *Ports of Call in Jamaica:*

Montego Bay:

Known for its lively atmosphere, Montego Bay offers stunning beaches, vibrant markets, and water activities. The cruise port is conveniently located near the city center.

Ocho Rios:

Famous for Dunn's River Falls, Ocho Rios is a haven for nature lovers. Cruise passengers can explore waterfalls, go zip-lining, or visit the nearby town of Fern Gully.

Falmouth:

Steeped in history, Falmouth boasts well-preserved Georgian architecture. Cruise passengers can explore historic sites, shop for local crafts, and sample Jamaican cuisine.

4. *Excursions and Attractions:*

Dunn's River Falls:

A must-visit natural attraction, Dunn's River Falls is a terraced waterfall that cascades over natural limestone stairs, providing an exhilarating climb for visitors.

Bob Marley Experience:

Reggae enthusiasts can opt for a tour to the birthplace and resting place of the legendary Bob Marley, experiencing the rich musical heritage of Jamaica.

Mystic Mountain:

Adventure seekers can embark on a journey to Mystic Mountain, where activities like bobsledding, zip-lining, and chairlift rides offer breathtaking views of the island.

5. Address Information:

Montego Bay Cruise Port:

Address: Montego Freeport, Montego Bay, Jamaica

Contact: +1 876-684-9901

Ocho Rios Cruise Port:

Address: Reynolds Pier, Main Street, Ocho Rios, Jamaica

Contact: +1 876-381-7654

Falmouth Cruise Port:

Address: Historic Falmouth Cruise Port, Falmouth, Jamaica

Contact: +1 876-634-1900

Embarking on a cruise to Jamaica opens up a world of adventure, from exploring cascading waterfalls to immersing oneself in the vibrant culture of the island. With diverse cruise lines and departure ports, travelers have the flexibility to choose the perfect itinerary that suits their preferences. Whether it's the lively beaches of Montego Bay or the natural wonders of Ocho Rios, a cruise to Jamaica promises an unforgettable Caribbean experience.

SECTION 3: DESTINATIONS

Kingston

Kingston, the vibrant capital of Jamaica, is a city that pulsates with life, culture, and history. Nestled on the southeastern coast of the island, Kingston serves as the cultural and economic heart of Jamaica. With its rich heritage, diverse population, and a blend of modernity and tradition, the city offers a captivating experience for visitors.

Kingston's history is deeply intertwined with the broader narrative of Jamaica's past. Originally founded in 1692 after a devastating earthquake destroyed the nearby city of Port Royal, Kingston became the new capital. Over the centuries, the city has evolved, reflecting the influences of Spanish, British, and African cultures. The historic district of Port Royal, known for its pirate lore and maritime history, is a short distance from Kingston and offers a fascinating glimpse into the island's colonial past.

The heartbeat of Kingston is undoubtedly its vibrant cultural scene. The city is a melting pot of artistic expression, with reggae music at its core. Visitors can immerse themselves in the rhythm of Jamaica by exploring the Bob Marley Museum, located in the legendary musician's former home. The museum provides insight into the life of this iconic reggae figure and the cultural movement he helped to shape.

Art enthusiasts will find solace in the National Gallery of Jamaica, a treasure trove of Caribbean art. From traditional to contemporary pieces, the gallery showcases the island's artistic evolution and the voices of its people.

Wandering through Kingston's bustling markets is an immersive experience. The Coronation Market, a hub of activity, offers a kaleidoscope of colors, sounds, and flavors. Here, locals and visitors alike can sample fresh fruits, spices, and local delicacies, creating a sensory journey through Jamaican cuisine.

Devon House, a historic mansion turned shopping and dining destination, provides a different ambiance. Its lush lawns and colonial architecture offer a serene escape from the urban bustle. Visitors can indulge in gourmet ice cream or explore the artisan shops within the premises.

Kingston's urban landscape is a juxtaposition of modern skyscrapers and colonial architecture. Emancipation Park, a green oasis in the heart of the city, invites both locals and tourists to relax

amid sculptures and fountains. The skyline of New Kingston, the city's central business district, is a testament to Jamaica's economic vitality.

For a panoramic view of Kingston and its harbor, visitors can ascend the Blue Mountains. The journey to the peak unveils not only breathtaking scenery but also the significance of coffee production in Jamaica. The Blue Mountain Coffee, revered globally for its rich flavor, has its roots in this region.

Jamaican cuisine is a delightful fusion of flavors, and Kingston is the perfect place to savor it. From the spicy jerk chicken to the savory patties, the city's culinary offerings are a testament to its diverse influences. Street-side vendors and upscale restaurants alike contribute to the gastronomic tapestry that defines Kingston's food scene.

Kingston is a city that captivates the senses and weaves together the threads of Jamaica's past and present. Its history, vibrant culture, bustling markets, urban landscapes, and culinary delights make it a must-visit destination for those seeking an authentic Jamaican experience. As the beating heart of the island, Kingston invites visitors to explore, discover, and immerse themselves in the rhythm of Jamaica.

Historical Sites in Kingston

Explore the following historical sites that showcase the evolution of this fascinating city.

1. *Devon House*

Address: 26 Hope Road, Kingston 10, Jamaica

Nestled in the heart of Kingston, Devon House is a well-preserved mansion dating back to the 19th century. Built in 1881, it was the residence of Jamaica's first black millionaire, George Stiebel. The mansion offers a glimpse into Jamaica's colonial past with its Georgian architecture, antique furniture, and lush gardens.

2. *Bob Marley Museum*

Address: 56 Hope Road, Kingston 6, Jamaica

Immerse yourself in the life and legacy of the legendary reggae icon, Bob Marley. The Bob Marley Museum is housed in the former residence of the reggae superstar and provides an

intimate look into his life, music, and the cultural movement he inspired. The museum showcases memorabilia, personal artifacts, and the studio where Marley recorded some of his most famous tracks.

3. *National Gallery of Jamaica*

Address: 12 Ocean Boulevard, Kingston, Jamaica

Located in the heart of downtown Kingston, the National Gallery of Jamaica is the country's premier art institution. It houses an extensive collection of Jamaican art, spanning from the Taino period to contemporary works. The gallery is a testament to Jamaica's artistic evolution, featuring paintings, sculptures, and multimedia installations.

4. *Spanish Town Square*

Address: Spanish Town, Kingston, Jamaica

Venture to Spanish Town, the former capital of Jamaica, and explore the historic Spanish Town Square. Surrounded by well-preserved Georgian architecture, the square was once a bustling hub during the island's colonial era. Highlights include the historic Rodney's Memorial and the Old Kings House, providing a window into Jamaica's colonial history.

5. Port Royal

Address: Port Royal, Kingston, Jamaica

Known as the "wickedest city on Earth" during the 17th century, Port Royal was a haven for pirates and buccaneers. Today, the archaeological remains of Port Royal offer a fascinating glimpse into the city's notorious past. Visit the Port Royal Archaeological Museum to learn about the earthquake that sank a portion of the city beneath the sea.

6. Institute of Jamaica

Address: 10-16 East Street, Kingston, Jamaica

The Institute of Jamaica, founded in 1879, is dedicated to preserving the cultural heritage of Jamaica. The museum houses exhibits on Jamaican music, science, and anthropology. It is also home to the Natural History Museum, the Jamaica Music Museum, and the National Museum Jamaica.

Kingston's historical sites weave a narrative that spans centuries, from the colonial period to the birth of reggae music. As you explore these sites, you'll gain a deeper understanding of Jamaica's diverse and resilient history. Make sure to take the time to immerse yourself in the stories and cultural richness that Kingston has to offer.

Dining and Nightlife in Kingston

Dining

1. **Devon House I-Scream**

Address: 26 Hope Road, Kingston

Start your culinary journey in Kingston with a visit to Devon House I-Scream. Located on the historic Devon House property, this ice cream parlor offers a delightful selection of locally inspired ice cream flavors. From the classic Rum and Raisin to the exotic Sour Sop, treat your taste buds to a cool and refreshing experience.

2. **Usain Bolt's Tracks and Records**

Address: Marketplace, 67 Constant Spring Rd, Kingston

For a taste of Jamaican and international cuisine in a vibrant atmosphere, head to Usain Bolt's Tracks and Records. Named after the world-renowned sprinter Usain Bolt, this sports bar and restaurant is a popular spot for both locals and visitors. Enjoy a diverse menu, including jerk chicken, patties, and a variety of cocktails.

3. **Toss and Roll Salad Bar**

Address: Sovereign North Shopping Centre, 29 Barbican Road, Kingston

Health-conscious travelers will appreciate Toss and Roll Salad Bar. This eatery offers a range of fresh and customizable salads, wraps, and smoothies. Whether you're a vegetarian or a meat lover, you'll find delicious options made from locally sourced ingredients.

4. **The Terra Nova All Suite Hotel**

Address: 17 Waterloo Road, Kingston

For an upscale dining experience, visit The Terra Nova All Suite Hotel. The hotel's restaurant boasts a diverse menu of international and Jamaican dishes, prepared with a gourmet touch. With its elegant ambiance and attentive service, it's an ideal choice for a special evening.

Nightlife

1. **Regency Bar and Lounge**

Address: Terra Nova All Suite Hotel, 17 Waterloo Road, Kingston

After a satisfying dinner at The Terra Nova, head to the Regency Bar and Lounge for a sophisticated nightcap. Enjoy signature cocktails and live entertainment in a stylish setting. The Regency Bar is perfect for those seeking a more relaxed and upscale nightlife experience.

2. **Fiction Fantasy Nightclub**

Address: Marketplace, 67 Constant Spring Rd, Kingston

If you're in the mood for dancing and lively music, Fiction Fantasy Nightclub is the place to be. This popular club features themed nights, a spacious dance floor, and a variety of music genres to keep the party going into the early morning hours.

3. **Puls8**

Address: Villa Ronai, Stony Hill, Kingston

Puls8, located in the picturesque hills of Stony Hill, offers a unique and upscale nightlife experience. With its outdoor terrace and stunning views of Kingston, it's a favorite among locals for its chic ambiance and diverse music selection.

4. **Redbones Blues Café**

Address: 1 Argyle Road, Kingston

For a more laid-back evening, visit Redbones Blues Café. This venue combines live music performances with a cozy atmosphere. Whether you're into jazz, blues, or reggae, Redbones offers a relaxed space to enjoy great music and good company.

Resorts and Hotels in Kingston

From luxurious resorts to charming boutique hotels, visitors can find the perfect place to stay while exploring the city's rich culture and history. Here are some noteworthy options:

1. **Spanish Court Hotel**

Address: 1 St. Lucia Avenue, Kingston

Description: Spanish Court Hotel is a contemporary and stylish hotel located in the heart of New Kingston. With modern amenities, spacious rooms, and excellent service, it caters to both business and leisure travelers. The hotel features a rooftop pool, fitness center, and a variety of dining options.

2. **The Jamaica Pegasus Hotel**

Address: 81 Knutsford Boulevard, Kingston

Description: Situated in the heart of the business and financial district, The Jamaica Pegasus Hotel is a landmark in Kingston. Boasting a blend of classic elegance and modern comfort, this hotel offers spacious rooms, a spa, multiple dining options, and conference facilities.

3. **The Jamaica Inn**

Address: 2-4 Ruthven Road, Kingston

Description: The Jamaica Inn is a boutique hotel that combines Jamaican charm with a relaxed atmosphere. Set amidst lush gardens, it provides a peaceful retreat within the bustling city. Guests can enjoy personalized service, elegant rooms, and a poolside bar.

4. **Courtyard by Marriott Kingston**

Address: 1 Park Close, Kingston

Description: Courtyard by Marriott Kingston offers a blend of comfort and functionality. Conveniently located, this hotel is designed for both business and leisure travelers. It features modern rooms, a fitness center, and a restaurant serving international cuisine.

5. **Altamont Court Hotel**

Address: 1-5 Altamont Terrace, Kingston

Description: Altamont Court Hotel is a budget-friendly option offering a comfortable stay in New Kingston. With a focus on personalized service, the hotel provides cozy rooms, a restaurant serving local and international dishes, and a pool for relaxation.

6. ***Spanish Gardens Hotel***

Address: 4 East Kirkland Heights, Kingston

Description: Spanish Gardens Hotel is a hidden gem in the hills of Kingston. Nestled in a tranquil setting, it offers panoramic views of the city. The hotel provides intimate and personalized service, making it an ideal choice for those seeking a quiet retreat.

Whether you're looking for luxury, convenience, or a more intimate experience, Kingston has a range of resorts and hotels to cater to diverse preferences. Before making reservations, it's advisable to check recent reviews, amenities, and any special offers each accommodation may provide. Additionally, confirm the accuracy of addresses and contact information to ensure a smooth and enjoyable stay in Kingston.

Hostels in Kingston: A Backpacker's Haven

Kingston, the vibrant capital of Jamaica, is a destination that offers not only cultural richness but also budget-friendly accommodation options for travelers seeking immersive experiences. Hostels, in particular, provide a unique opportunity to connect with fellow adventurers while exploring the city's wonders. Here's a guide to some notable hostels in Kingston, complete with addresses for your convenience.

1. ***Reggae Hostel Kingston***

Address: 8 Burlington Ave, Kingston, Jamaica

Located in the heart of New Kingston, Reggae Hostel is a popular choice for budget-conscious travelers. The hostel boasts colorful décor, a laid-back atmosphere, and friendly staff. With both dormitory-style and private rooms available, it caters to a variety of preferences. The communal spaces are ideal for meeting fellow travelers, and the hostel often hosts events to enhance the social experience.

2. Pegasus Hostel Kingston

Address: 22 Hopefield Ave, Kingston, Jamaica

Situated in a central location, Pegasus Hostel offers budget accommodation without compromising on comfort. The hostel features spacious dormitories and private rooms, ensuring a good night's rest after a day of exploring Kingston. With a communal kitchen and cozy common areas, Pegasus Hostel encourages a sense of community among guests.

3. The Durham Hostel

Address: 4 Durham Ave, Kingston, Jamaica

Nestled in the historic neighborhood of Half-Way-Tree, The Durham Hostel provides a charming and relaxed environment for backpackers. The hostel's proximity to local markets and cultural attractions makes it an excellent choice for those eager to experience Kingston's authenticity. The Durham Hostel emphasizes a sustainable and eco-friendly approach to travel.

4. Chez Nous Corporate

Address: 6 Latham Ave, Kingston, Jamaica

Offering a blend of affordability and convenience, Chez Nous Corporate is a budget-friendly accommodation option in Kingston. The hostel provides a range of room options, including dormitory-style and private rooms. Its strategic location near major transportation hubs makes it an ideal choice for travelers exploring the city and beyond.

5. The View Hostel

Address: 6 Blithewood Ave, Kingston, Jamaica

As the name suggests, The View Hostel offers stunning panoramic views of Kingston. Located in the cool hills of St. Andrew, this hostel provides a tranquil retreat from the hustle and bustle of the city. With a mix of dormitories and private rooms, The View Hostel is known for its welcoming atmosphere and engaging activities for guests.

Kingston's hostels not only offer budget-friendly accommodations but also serve as hubs for cultural exchange and adventure. Whether you're a solo traveler or part of a group, these hostels provide a welcoming haven for those looking to explore the dynamic city of Kingston without breaking the bank. Make sure to check each hostel's website or contact them directly for the most up-to-date information on availability and amenities. Enjoy your stay in Kingston!

Shopping in Kingston: A Retail Paradise in Jamaica

From bustling markets to upscale boutiques, Kingston offers a shopping experience that caters to every taste and budget. In this guide, we will explore the best shopping spots in Kingston, providing you with addresses to ensure you find your way to these retail havens.

1. **Devon House Craft Market**

*Address: 26 Hope Road, K*Kingsto

The Devon House Craft Market is a treasure trove of Jamaican craftsmanship. Located on the grounds of the historic Devon House, this market features stalls selling handmade jewelry, traditional clothing, and unique souvenirs. Take a leisurely stroll through the market, interact with local artisans, and pick up one-of-a-kind items that reflect the island's artistic spirit.

2. **Half-Way-Tree Square**

Address: Half-Way-Tree, Kingston

For a more mainstream shopping experience, Half-Way-Tree Square is the go-to destination. This bustling commercial area is home to numerous shops, boutiques, and department stores. From international brands to local designers, you'll find a wide array of clothing, accessories,

and electronics. Don't forget to explore the vibrant street market where local vendors showcase their goods.

3. Craft Cottage

Address: 8 Central Avenue, Kingston

Craft Cottage is a quaint store located in the heart of Kingston, offering a curated selection of Jamaican handicrafts. This boutique is a haven for those seeking authentic gifts and souvenirs. From handmade pottery to intricately woven baskets, Craft Cottage celebrates the skill and creativity of local artisans.

4. MegaMart

Address: 29 Upper Waterloo Road, Kingston

If you're looking for a one-stop shopping experience, MegaMart is the place to be. This large supermarket offers a wide range of products, including groceries, clothing, electronics, and household items. It's a convenient option for both locals and tourists looking to stock up on essentials or indulge in some retail therapy.

5. The Pegasus Mall

Address: 81 Knutsford Boulevard, Kingston

Situated within the luxurious Jamaica Pegasus Hotel, The Pegasus Mall caters to those with a taste for upscale shopping. Explore designer boutiques, jewelry stores, and specialty shops offering high-end products. After a day of shopping, unwind at one of the mall's chic cafes or restaurants.

6. Coronation Market

Address: Pechon Street, Kingston

For an authentic Jamaican market experience, head to Coronation Market. Located in downtown Kingston, this bustling market is a sensory delight with vibrant colors, exotic fruits, and the rhythmic sounds of bargaining. It's the perfect place to immerse yourself in the local culture and purchase fresh produce, spices, and handmade crafts.

7. **Taj Mahal Shopping Centre**

Address: 78 Main Street, Kingston

Taj Mahal Shopping Centre is a landmark in Kingston, known for its diverse range of shops. From clothing stores to electronics outlets, this shopping center caters to a wide range of tastes. The lively atmosphere and variety of goods make it a popular choice for both locals and visitors.

Kingston's shopping scene is as diverse as the city itself, offering a mix of traditional markets, upscale boutiques, and modern shopping centers. Whether you're in search of handmade crafts, designer clothing, or fresh produce, Kingston has it all. Use this guide with addresses to navigate the city's shopping landscape and indulge in a retail experience that reflects the vibrant spirit of Jamaica. Happy shopping!

Beaches and Water Activities in Kingston: A Tropical Paradise Unveiled

When one thinks of Kingston, the bustling capital of Jamaica, images of vibrant street markets, reggae beats, and historical sites may come to mind. However, beyond the city's cultural richness lies a coastal haven waiting to be explored. Kingston boasts some of the most picturesque beaches and a plethora of water activities that cater to both relaxation seekers and adventure enthusiasts. In this guide, we'll delve into the sun-soaked shores, crystal-clear waters, and exciting water-based adventures that make Kingston a tropical paradise.

1. **Hellshire Beach**

Situated approximately 25 kilometers south of Kingston, Hellshire Beach is a local gem renowned for its golden sands and warm, inviting waters. This stretch of coastline is not only a favorite among locals for weekend getaways but also draws visitors seeking an authentic Jamaican beach experience.

Water Activities:

Swimming: The calm and shallow waters make Hellshire Beach an ideal spot for a refreshing swim.

Seafood Delights: Indulge in local seafood delights from the vibrant beachside shacks.

Address:

Hellshire Beach, Portmore, St. Catherine, Jamaica

2. Lime Cay

For those yearning for a more secluded and pristine escape, Lime Cay, a small uninhabited island off the coast of Kingston, is the answer. Accessible only by boat, this hidden paradise offers tranquility away from the bustling mainland.

Water Activities:

Snorkeling: Explore the vibrant underwater world surrounding Lime Cay.

Boat Tours: Hire a local boat for a personalized tour of the area.

Address:

Lime Cay, Kingston, Jamaica (Accessible by boat from Morgan's Harbour)

3. Fort Clarence Beach

Combining history with natural beauty, Fort Clarence Beach stands as a testament to Jamaica's rich past. The remnants of an old fort overlook the beach, adding a touch of historical charm to this popular destination.

Water Activities:

Jet Skiing: Experience the thrill of jet skiing along the coast.

Volleyball: Engage in a friendly game of beach volleyball with locals and fellow tourists.

Address:

Fort Clarence Beach, Hellshire, Portmore, St. Catherine, Jamaica

4. Port Royal

Once a haven for pirates, Port Royal now invites travelers to explore its history and enjoy its stunning waterfront. The picturesque beaches offer a blend of relaxation and adventure, making it an ideal spot for a day trip.

Water Activities:

Dolphin Watching: Embark on a boat tour for a chance to spot dolphins in the Caribbean Sea.

Historical Tours: Discover the intriguing history of Port Royal with guided tours.

Address:

Port Royal, Kingston, Jamaica

5. Blue Mountains and John Crow Mountains National Park

While not a traditional beach destination, the Blue Mountains and John Crow Mountains National Park offer a unique water-centric experience. Hidden waterfalls, cool mountain streams, and lush greenery create a serene escape from the coastal heat.

Water Activities:

Hiking to Waterfalls: Trek through the mountains to discover hidden waterfalls like Reach Falls.

Bird Watching: Explore the diverse bird species around the mountain streams.

Address:

Blue Mountains and John Crow Mountains National Park, Jamaica

Kingston's beaches and water activities unveil a different facet of this vibrant city. Whether you're looking for a tranquil day by the shore or an adventurous exploration of the underwater world, Kingston's coastal offerings are sure to leave you with memories of sun, sea, and smiles. So, pack your sunscreen, embrace the Jamaican spirit, and dive into the aquatic wonders that await in Kingston.

Montego Bay

Exploring Montego Bay's Rich History: A Journey Through Its Historical Sites

Montego Bay, a picturesque coastal town in Jamaica, is not only known for its stunning beaches and vibrant culture but also for its rich history. From colonial-era structures to landmarks that played pivotal roles in the island's past, Montego Bay's historical sites offer a captivating journey through time. In this guide, we'll delve into the heart of Montego Bay's history, exploring its most notable historical sites and uncovering the stories they hold.

1. **Rose Hall Great House**

Location: Rose Hall, Montego Bay

History: Dating back to the 18th century, the Rose Hall Great House stands as a symbol of Jamaica's plantation era. Once home to the infamous Annie Palmer, the "White Witch of Rose Hall," the mansion is shrouded in tales of mystery and intrigue.

Architecture: Explore the Georgian architecture of the Great House, showcasing the grandeur of the sugar plantation era.

Guided Tours: Visitors can take guided tours, delving into the history of Rose Hall and the legends that surround it.

2. **Sam Sharpe Square**

Location: Downtown Montego Bay

History: Named after the national hero and leader of the 1831 Christmas Rebellion, Sam Sharpe, this square is a historical hub. Learn about Sharpe's legacy and the role he played in the fight for emancipation.

Monuments: Discover the monuments and statues honoring key figures in Jamaica's history, including Sam Sharpe and other freedom fighters.

Local Culture: Explore the vibrant local culture around the square, with shops, markets, and street performances.

3. The Cage

Location: Harbour Street, Montego Bay

History: Known as "The Cage," this small but significant structure was once used as a holding area for runaway slaves. Delve into the dark history of slavery in Jamaica and the resilience of those who sought freedom.

Preservation Efforts: Learn about preservation efforts and initiatives aimed at maintaining this historical site for future generations.

4. Montego Bay Civic Centre

Location: Sam Sharpe Square

History: Housed in a former courthouse, the Montego Bay Civic Centre boasts a rich history tied to Jamaica's legal system. Explore the architecture and historical artifacts within its walls.

Exhibitions: Discover rotating exhibitions that showcase Montego Bay's history, including its colonial past, struggles for independence, and cultural evolution.

5. St. James Parish Church

Location: Gloucester Avenue, Montego Bay

History: As one of the oldest churches in Jamaica, St. James Parish Church dates back to the 18th century. Explore its architectural beauty and learn about its role in the religious and social fabric of Montego Bay.

Cemetery: Wander through the church's cemetery, where historic tombstones tell stories of individuals who shaped the community.

6. Fort Montego

Location: St. James Street, Montego Bay

History: Built in the early 18th century by the British, Fort Montego stands as a testament to Jamaica's strategic importance during times of war. Uncover the military history of the fort and its role in defending the island.

Montego Bay's historical sites provide a fascinating glimpse into Jamaica's past, from the days of colonial rule to the struggles for freedom and independence. As you explore these landmarks,

you not only witness the architectural beauty but also feel the echoes of the stories embedded in their walls. Whether you're a history enthusiast or a casual traveler, Montego Bay's historical sites offer a journey through time, inviting you to connect with the island's vibrant and complex heritage.

Dining and Nightlife in Montego Bay: A Culinary and Entertainment Extravaganza

Montego Bay, often referred to as MoBay, is not only known for its stunning beaches and vibrant culture but also for its diverse and delectable culinary scene and lively nightlife. Visitors to Montego Bay can embark on a gastronomic journey that ranges from traditional Jamaican flavors to international cuisine. When the sun sets, the city comes alive with a pulsating nightlife that caters to a variety of tastes. Below is a detailed exploration of the dining and nightlife options in Montego Bay.

Dining in Montego Bay

Traditional Jamaican Cuisine
Montego Bay boasts an array of restaurants that showcase the rich and flavorful Jamaican cuisine. From jerk chicken to curried goat, visitors can savor the authenticity of local dishes. Here are some must-try restaurants:

Scotchies Jerk Center
Address: Kent Avenue, Montego Bay
Dive into the heart of Jamaican flavors with Scotchies Jerk Center, known for its mouthwatering jerk chicken and pork. The open-air setting adds to the laid-back experience.

The Pelican Grill

Address: Gloucester Avenue, Montego Bay

Enjoy a waterfront dining experience at The Pelican Grill, offering a mix of Jamaican and international cuisine. The seafood dishes are a highlight, prepared with a local twist.

International Cuisine

For those seeking a diverse culinary experience, Montego Bay has a range of restaurants serving international fare.

Marguerite's

Address: Gloucester Avenue, Montego Bay

Indulge in fine dining at Marguerite's, featuring a menu that combines French and Jamaican influences. The elegant ambiance is perfect for a romantic evening.

Mystic India

Address: Fairview Shopping Center, Montego Bay

Spice up your taste buds with authentic Indian cuisine at Mystic India. The restaurant offers a selection of curries, tandoori dishes, and delectable desserts.

Beachfront Dining

Montego Bay's coastal location allows for stunning beachfront dining experiences.

The Houseboat Grill

Address: Alice Eldemire Drive, Freeport, Montego Bay

Set on a floating restaurant, The Houseboat Grill offers a unique dining experience. Enjoy seafood and international dishes while surrounded by the serene waters of Montego Bay.

Pier One

Address: Howard Cooke Boulevard, Montego Bay

Known for its seafood and Jamaican specialties, Pier One provides a lively atmosphere with both indoor and outdoor seating. The restaurant often features live music.

Nightlife in Montego Bay

Beach Bars and Lounges

As the sun sets, Montego Bay transforms into a hub of nightlife activities. Beach bars and lounges offer a perfect blend of relaxation and entertainment.

Jimmy Buffett's Margaritaville

Address: Gloucester Avenue, Montego Bay

Embrace the tropical vibe at Margaritaville, where you can enjoy cocktails, music, and even water activities. The lively atmosphere makes it a popular spot for both locals and tourists.

Doctor's Cave Beach Club

Address: Gloucester Avenue, Montego Bay

Experience nightlife on the beach at Doctor's Cave Beach Club. The beach bar provides a relaxed setting with live music, making it an ideal place to unwind.

Resorts and Hotels in Montego Bay: A Luxurious Escape

When it comes to accommodation, Montego Bay offers an array of resorts and hotels that cater to every traveler's needs. Whether you're seeking a romantic getaway, a family-friendly retreat, or a luxury escape, Montego Bay has something for everyone.

1. Tranquil Retreats

a. Half Moon, Rose Hall

Address: Rose Hall, Montego Bay, Jamaica

Nestled on a sprawling 400-acre estate, Half Moon is a haven of luxury. With its colonial-style architecture and world-class amenities, this resort offers a blend of old-world charm and modern elegance. Guests can enjoy a private beach, championship golf courses, and an award-winning spa.

b. Round Hill Hotel and Villas

Address: John Pringle Drive, Montego Bay, Jamaica

Perched on a lush hillside, Round Hill Hotel and Villas is an iconic retreat known for its understated luxury. The resort features boutique oceanfront villas, each uniquely decorated by renowned designers. With a private beach, exceptional dining, and a spa, Round Hill provides an intimate and serene escape.

2. Family-Friendly Escapes

a. Hilton Rose Hall Resort & Spa

Address: Rose Hall Main Road, Montego Bay, Jamaica

Hilton Rose Hall Resort & Spa is a family-friendly haven, offering a water park, kid's club, and spacious accommodations. The resort's All-Inclusive option makes it easy for families to enjoy meals, activities, and entertainment without worrying about additional costs.

b. Iberostar Selection Rose Hall Suites

Address: Rose Hall Main Road, Montego Bay, Jamaica

Catering to families, Iberostar Selection Rose Hall Suites combines luxury and entertainment. The resort boasts spacious suites, multiple pools, and a splash park for children. Parents can indulge in spa treatments or enjoy the resort's diverse dining options.

3. All-Inclusive Luxury

a. Secrets St. James Montego Bay

Address: Lot 59A Freeport, Montego Bay, Jamaica

For adults seeking an exclusive and romantic escape, Secrets St. James Montego Bay is an ideal choice. This all-inclusive, adults-only resort offers gourmet dining, premium beverages, and a range of activities. Guests can relax in private cabanas by the pool or unwind at the world-class spa.

b. Excellence Oyster Bay

Address: Peninsula Falmouth, Montego Bay, Jamaica

Located on a private peninsula, Excellence Oyster Bay is a luxury, all-inclusive resort known for its impeccable service and attention to detail. With overwater bungalows, a variety of dining options, and a full-service spa, this resort provides an indulgent experience for discerning travelers.

5. Boutique Bliss

a. S Hotel Jamaica

Address: 7 Jimmy Cliff Boulevard, Montego Bay, Jamaica

The trendy S Hotel Jamaica offers a boutique experience with stylish design and personalized service. Located on the famous Doctor's Cave Beach, the hotel provides a chic and intimate atmosphere, complemented by rooftop dining and a beach club.

b. The Cliff Hotel

Address: West End Road, Negril, Montego Bay, Jamaica

While not directly in Montego Bay, The Cliff Hotel in nearby Negril is worth mentioning. Perched on the cliffs, this boutique hotel offers panoramic views of the Caribbean Sea. With its elegant design, cliffside dining, and personalized service, The Cliff Hotel provides a unique and romantic escape.

Hostels in Montego Bay: A Backpacker's Haven

For those looking for affordable and sociable accommodation, hostels in Montego Bay provide an excellent option. Here's an exploration of some noteworthy hostels, complete with addresses to make your stay memorable.

1. **Reggae Hostel Montego Bay**

Address: 6 Mary's Bay, Freeport, Montego Bay, Jamaica

Nestled in the heart of Montego Bay, the Reggae Hostel offers a perfect blend of budget-friendly prices and a lively atmosphere. The hostel provides both dormitory-style and private rooms, giving travelers the flexibility to choose based on their preferences. With its central location, guests can easily explore nearby attractions such as the Hip Strip and Doctor's Cave Beach.

2. **MoBay Hostel**

Address: 47 Union Street, Montego Bay, Jamaica

MoBay Hostel is a cozy and welcoming option for backpackers. Its location near the city center makes it convenient for exploring local markets, restaurants, and historical sites. The hostel's communal areas encourage socializing, and the friendly staff often organize group activities, creating a sense of community among guests.

3. **Paradise Backpackers**

Address: 51 Gloucester Avenue, Montego Bay, Jamaica

Situated along the picturesque Gloucester Avenue, Paradise Backpackers is an ideal choice for those who want to be close to the beach and nightlife. The hostel boasts colorful and comfortable dormitories and common spaces where travelers can share stories and make new friends. The lively atmosphere makes it a popular spot for solo travelers looking to connect with fellow adventurers.

4. **Hip Strip Backpackers Hostel**

Address: 34 Queens Drive, Montego Bay, Jamaica

As the name suggests, Hip Strip Backpackers Hostel is located along the famous Hip Strip, offering easy access to shops, bars, and entertainment venues. The hostel's laid-back vibe and budget-friendly accommodations make it a favorite among backpackers. The staff is known for their warm hospitality, providing guests with valuable insights into local gems.

5. **Montego Bay Club Hostel**

Address: 11 Queens Drive, Montego Bay, Jamaica

Montego Bay Club Hostel provides a mix of affordability and comfort. With its close proximity to the beach and popular attractions, this hostel is an excellent choice for those who want to explore Montego Bay without breaking the bank. The on-site facilities, including a communal kitchen and social areas, enhance the overall backpacker experience.

Montego Bay's hostels offer budget-conscious travelers the opportunity to immerse themselves in the local culture while enjoying the camaraderie of like-minded adventurers. Whether you prefer the lively atmosphere of the Hip Strip or a more relaxed setting near the beach, Montego Bay's hostels cater to a range of preferences, making your Jamaican journey both affordable and memorable.

A Shopper's Paradise: Exploring Montego Bay's Vibrant Retail Scene

Montego Bay caters to a diverse range of tastes and preferences. This guide will lead you through the bustling shopping districts, highlighting key addresses to ensure your retail journey is nothing short of extraordinary.

1. Hip Strip – Gloucester Avenue

1.1 Duty-Free Shopping at City Centre Plaza

Begin your shopping spree on Gloucester Avenue, popularly known as the "Hip Strip." The City Centre Plaza is a duty-free haven, offering an array of luxury items, from jewelry and watches to high-end fashion. Address: City Centre Plaza, 4-14 Harbour Street, Montego Bay.

1.2 Craft Market for Authentic Souvenirs

Adjacent to the City Centre Plaza is the Craft Market, a vibrant hub where local artisans showcase their craftsmanship. Dive into a sea of handcrafted souvenirs, including wood carvings, straw hats, and vibrant textiles. Address: Gloucester Avenue Craft Market, Hip Strip, Montego Bay.

2. The Shoppes at Rose Hall

2.1 Luxury Brands and Fine Dining

For a taste of upscale shopping, head to The Shoppes at Rose Hall. This premier shopping destination features renowned international brands, duty-free outlets, and an assortment of fine dining options. Address: The Shoppes at Rose Hall, Rose Hall Main Road, Montego Bay.

3. Old Fort Craft Park

3.1 Artisanal Delights with Historical Charm

Located within the historic Montego Bay Cultural Centre, the Old Fort Craft Park is a treasure trove of artisanal creations. Browse through local paintings, handmade jewelry, and traditional Jamaican crafts. Address: Old Fort Craft Park, 2-4 Fort Street, Montego Bay.

4. Fairview Shopping Centre

4.1 Retail Therapy and Entertainment

Indulge in a diverse shopping experience at the Fairview Shopping Centre, where international and local brands coexist. With an array of shops, restaurants, and a cinema, it's the perfect place

for retail therapy and entertainment. Address: Fairview Shopping Centre, Alice Eldemire Drive, Montego Bay.

5. Sam Sharpe Square

5.1 Historic Charm and Local Vendors

Step into the heart of Montego Bay's historic district at Sam Sharpe Square. Amidst colonial architecture, discover local vendors selling an assortment of goods, from handmade crafts to traditional Jamaican spices. Address: Sam Sharpe Square, Downtown Montego Bay.

6. Half Moon Shopping Village

6.1 Boutique Bliss in a Resort Setting

If you seek a blend of boutique shopping and a resort atmosphere, the Half Moon Shopping Village is the place to be. Explore a curated selection of shops offering fashion, jewelry, and unique souvenirs. Address: Half Moon Shopping Village, Half Moon, Rose Hall, Montego Bay.

Montego Bay's shopping scene is as diverse as the island's rich culture. From bustling craft markets to upscale shopping centers, each retail destination offers a unique glimpse into Jamaica's vibrant heritage. So, whether you're looking for duty-free luxury or handcrafted souvenirs, Montego Bay promises a shopper's paradise.

Explore these addresses, immerse yourself in the local culture, and return home with not just memories of the sun-soaked beaches but also with bags filled with the essence of Jamaica. Happy shopping!

Discovering Paradise: Beaches and Water Activities in Montego Bay

Montego Bay, a gem nestled on the northwestern coast of Jamaica, is renowned for its pristine beaches and vibrant water activities. Whether you seek relaxation on the sandy shores or crave the thrill of aquatic adventures, Montego Bay has something for every beach enthusiast. Let's embark on a journey to explore the sun-soaked beaches and exciting water activities that make Montego Bay a tropical haven.

1. ***Doctor's Cave Beach Club***

Address: Gloucester Avenue, Montego Bay, Jamaica

Kick off your beach exploration at the iconic Doctor's Cave Beach Club. With its powdery white sand and crystal-clear turquoise waters, this beach has been a magnet for locals and tourists alike for decades. The beach club offers amenities like beach umbrellas, lounge chairs, and water sports equipment rentals.

Water Activities:

Snorkeling: Explore the vibrant marine life just off the shore.

Glass-Bottom Boat Tours: Witness the underwater wonders without getting wet.

2. ***Walter Fletcher Beach***

Address: Walter Fletcher Beach Road, Montego Bay, Jamaica

Walter Fletcher Beach, adjacent to the Aquasol Theme Park, is a family-friendly destination. The golden sand stretches along the coastline, offering a perfect spot for picnics and sunbathing. The beach is well-maintained, and its calm waters make it suitable for swimmers of all ages.

Water Activities:

Pedal Boating: Enjoy a leisurely ride along the tranquil waters.

Jet Skiing: Feel the adrenaline rush as you skim the waves.

3. Cornwall Beach

Address: Kent Avenue, Montego Bay, Jamaica

Cornwall Beach is a hidden gem known for its relaxed atmosphere and scenic beauty. The calm, shallow waters make it an excellent choice for families with young children. The beach is less crowded compared to others, providing a more intimate experience.

Water Activities:

Beach Volleyball: Join in a friendly game on the well-maintained courts.

Kayaking: Paddle along the shoreline and enjoy the coastal views.

4. AquaSol Theme Park

Address: Gloucester Avenue, Montego Bay, Jamaica

AquaSol Theme Park is an all-in-one destination for water enthusiasts. Besides the sandy beach, the park features a range of water-based attractions, making it a perfect spot for those seeking excitement and adventure.

Water Activities:

Water Trampolines: Bounce on the water for a fun-filled experience.

Parasailing: Soar above Montego Bay and savor breathtaking views.

5. Rose Hall Beach

Address: Rose Hall, Montego Bay, Jamaica

Situated near the historic Rose Hall Great House, Rose Hall Beach offers a blend of history and natural beauty. The beach boasts golden sand and is surrounded by lush greenery, providing a picturesque setting for a day in the sun.

Water Activities:

Windsurfing: Harness the power of the wind for an exhilarating ride.

Stand-Up Paddleboarding: Glide along the coastline on a paddleboard.

6. Dead End Beach

Address: Dead End, Montego Bay, Jamaica

For those seeking a more secluded escape, Dead End Beach is the answer. Tucked away from the bustling tourist spots, this beach offers tranquility and a sense of serenity. The shallow, clear waters make it ideal for leisurely swims.

Water Activities:

Snorkeling Excursions: Discover the vibrant underwater world with guided tours.

Fishing: Try your hand at traditional Jamaican fishing techniques.

7. Montego Bay Marine Park

Address: Howard Cooke Boulevard, Montego Bay, Jamaica

Nature and adventure collide at the Montego Bay Marine Park. This protected area encompasses various marine ecosystems, including coral reefs and seagrass beds. It's a haven for snorkelers and divers eager to explore Jamaica's diverse underwater landscapes.

Water Activities:

Snorkeling Trails: Follow marked trails to witness the marine biodiversity.

Scuba Diving: Dive into the depths and encounter colorful coral formations.

8. James Bond Beach

Address: Oracabessa, St Mary, Jamaica (Approximately 20 miles east of Montego Bay)

While not directly in Montego Bay, James Bond Beach is worth the journey. Famous for being featured in James Bond films, this beach offers a mix of history and allure. The clear waters and scenic surroundings create a mesmerizing atmosphere.

Water Activities:

Seafood Dining Cruise: Combine a culinary experience with a cruise along the coast.

Beach Volleyball Tournaments: Join or spectate thrilling beach volleyball matches.

9. **Falmouth Blue Waters Beach**

Address: Falmouth, Trelawny, Jamaica (Approximately 18 miles east of Montego Bay)

Venture a bit east of Montego Bay to discover the charm of Falmouth Blue Waters Beach. The calm waters and inviting ambiance make it a favorite among both locals and tourists. The beach is well-maintained, and the facilities cater to a range of preferences.

Water Activities:

Snorkel Safaris: Explore nearby reefs with expert guides.

Water Aerobics Classes: Stay active and have fun with organized water aerobics.

Montego Bay's beaches and water activities present a world of possibilities for every type of traveler. Whether you seek relaxation, adventure, or a bit of both, the diverse offerings of Montego Bay's coastal gems ensure an unforgettable experience. So, pack your sunscreen, don your swimsuit, and get ready to dive into the splendor of Jamaica's aquatic paradise.

Ocho Rios

Historical Sites in Ocho Rios: Exploring Jamaica's Rich Heritage

Ocho Rios, a picturesque town on Jamaica's north coast, is not only famous for its stunning beaches and lush landscapes but also boasts a rich historical heritage. As you embark on a journey through the historical sites in Ocho Rios, you'll discover a tapestry of stories that shaped the region. From colonial relics to cultural landmarks, each site provides a glimpse into Jamaica's

past. In this comprehensive guide, we'll delve into the fascinating historical sites in Ocho Rios, complete with addresses to ensure you can explore these treasures with ease.

1. *Columbus Park (Discovery Bay)*

Nestled in the heart of Discovery Bay, Columbus Park stands as a testament to Jamaica's encounter with Christopher Columbus in 1494. The park is home to several artifacts and monuments, including a water wheel and the Spanish Seville Cathedral. Visitors can explore the open-air museum and learn about the island's indigenous Taino people and the impact of European colonization.

Address: Columbus Park, Discovery Bay, St. Ann, Jamaica.

2. *Seville Great House and Heritage Park*

Immerse yourself in the colonial history of Jamaica by visiting the Seville Great House and Heritage Park. Built in the 18th century, this plantation house offers a glimpse into the island's past through its well-preserved architecture and exhibits. The Heritage Park surrounding the house features archaeological remains, showcasing the cultural complexity of Jamaica's history.

Address: Seville Great House, Priory St Ann, Jamaica.

3. *Firefly (Sir Noël Coward's Former Residence)*

Perched atop a hill with breathtaking views of Ocho Rios, Firefly was the former residence of the renowned playwright and composer Sir Noël Coward. This historical site provides a glimpse into the glamorous life of Coward and his notable guests, including Queen Elizabeth II. The house is now a museum, showcasing Coward's personal artifacts and offering a unique perspective on Jamaica's cultural history.

Address: Firefly, Oracabessa, St. Mary, Jamaica.

4. Rio Nuevo Battle Site

For those interested in military history, a visit to the Rio Nuevo Battle Site is a must. This location was the site of a significant battle between the Spanish and the English in 1658. Explore the museum and the battlefield, where artifacts and exhibits tell the story of this pivotal moment in Jamaica's history.

Address: Rio Nuevo Battle Site, St. Mary, Jamaica.

5. Tower Isle Fort

Built in the 18th century, Tower Isle Fort stands as a silent sentinel along Jamaica's coastline. Originally constructed to protect against pirate invasions, the fort offers panoramic views of the Caribbean Sea. Explore the well-preserved cannons and military structures that harken back to a time when the island faced the constant threat of maritime attacks.

Address: Tower Isle Fort, Tower Isle, St. Mary, Jamaica.

6. Green Grotto Caves

While primarily known for their natural beauty, the Green Grotto Caves also have historical significance. Used by the indigenous Taino people, the caves later served as a hideout for runaway slaves and a location for storing rum during the Spanish colonization. Guided tours take visitors through the labyrinthine passages, providing insights into the diverse historical uses of the caves.

Address: Green Grotto Caves, Discovery Bay, St. Ann, Jamaica.

As you explore the historical sites in Ocho Rios, you'll gain a deeper understanding of Jamaica's vibrant past. From the encounters with Christopher Columbus to the colonial legacy and the tales of battles, each site contributes to the mosaic of Jamaican history. Make sure to include these addresses in your itinerary to ensure a seamless journey through the captivating historical sites that Ocho Rios has to offer.

Dining and Nightlife in Ocho Rios

Dining

　　1. Scotchies Jerk Center

Address: Main Street, Ocho Rios

Renowned for its authentic Jamaican jerk cuisine, Scotchies Jerk Center is a must-visit for those looking to indulge in the bold flavors of the island. From succulent jerk chicken to flavorful pork, this open-air eatery provides a true taste of Jamaica. The laid-back atmosphere and aromatic grilling pits make it a favorite among both locals and tourists.

　　2. Evita's Italian Restaurant

Address: Eden Bower Road, Ocho Rios

For a change of pace, Evita's Italian Restaurant offers a fine dining experience with a spectacular view. Nestled on the hills overlooking Ocho Rios, this restaurant combines traditional Italian dishes with Jamaican flair. The extensive wine list and intimate setting make it ideal for a romantic evening or a special celebration.

　　3. Miss T's Kitchen

Address: Main Street, Ocho Rios

Miss T's Kitchen is a local gem, celebrated for its home-style Jamaican cooking. The menu features a variety of dishes made from fresh, locally sourced ingredients. From traditional breakfast options to hearty dinners, this cozy spot captures the essence of Jamaican hospitality. Don't miss the chance to try their famous 'Jerk Chicken Alfredo.'

　　4. Margaritaville Ocho Rios

Address: Island Village, Ocho Rios

Looking for a lively atmosphere? Head to Margaritaville for a blend of delicious food and entertainment. With a menu featuring a mix of Caribbean and international cuisine, this restaurant seamlessly transitions into a vibrant nightlife spot as the evening progresses. Enjoy live music, themed parties, and their signature margaritas.

Nightlife

1. Amnesia Nightclub

Address: Turtle River Road, Ocho Rios

Amnesia Nightclub is the go-to spot for those seeking a pulsating nightlife experience. With top-notch DJs, energetic dance floors, and a variety of themed nights, Amnesia ensures a memorable night out. The club attracts both locals and visitors, making it a melting pot of diverse music and dance styles.

2. Jimmy Buffett's Margaritaville

Address: Island Village, Ocho Rios

As the sun sets, Margaritaville transforms from a restaurant into a lively entertainment hub. The beachside location, live music, and an array of tropical cocktails set the stage for a relaxed yet vibrant evening. Join in the fun with their interactive bar staff and themed events.

3. Oceans 11

Address: Main Street, Ocho Rios

Oceans 11 is a beachfront bar offering a laid-back atmosphere with stunning views of the Caribbean Sea. Enjoy the sea breeze while sipping on tropical cocktails and listening to live music. This spot is perfect for those who prefer a more relaxed and intimate setting.

4. Pier 1

Address: Howard Cooke Highway, Ocho Rios

Located on a pier overlooking the water, Pier 1 is a versatile venue combining a restaurant, bar, and nightclub. The waterfront setting, live entertainment, and a diverse menu make it a popular choice for both dinner and late-night revelry. Check their event calendar for themed parties and special performances.

Ocho Rios offers a diverse culinary scene and a lively nightlife, catering to various tastes and preferences. Whether you're craving the bold flavors of jerk cuisine, seeking a romantic Italian dinner, or dancing the night away at a vibrant nightclub, Ocho Rios has something for everyone. Explore these dining and nightlife hotspots to make the most of your visit to this enchanting Jamaican destination.

Resorts and Hotels in Ocho Rios: A Tropical Haven

If you're planning a visit to this tropical paradise, choosing the right accommodation is crucial for an unforgettable experience. Here's a detailed look at some of the finest resorts and hotels in Ocho Rios, complete with their addresses.

1. ***Moon Palace Jamaica***

Address: Main Street, Ocho Rios

Description: Nestled between the scenic mountains and the Caribbean Sea, Moon Palace Jamaica offers a luxurious all-inclusive experience. With spacious rooms, multiple dining options, and a world-class spa, this resort is perfect for those seeking both relaxation and adventure.

2. ***Sandals Royal Plantation***

Address: Main Street, Ocho Rios

Description: A gem in the Sandals Resorts collection, Sandals Royal Plantation is an adults-only resort known for its impeccable service and breathtaking views. Set on a cliff overlooking the ocean, it provides a private and romantic atmosphere.

3. Jewel Dunn's River Beach Resort & Spa

Address: Mammee Bay, Ocho Rios

Description: This all-inclusive resort caters to adults and offers a blend of luxury and laid-back Jamaican charm. Enjoy the private beach, multiple restaurants, and the Radiant Spa for a truly rejuvenating stay.

4. Couples Tower Isle

Address: Tower Isle, Ocho Rios

Description: An award-winning, adults-only resort, Couples Tower Isle boasts a pristine private beach and a variety of water sports. The resort's design reflects the glamour of the 1950s, creating a unique and romantic ambiance.

5. Mystic Ridge Resort

Address: DaCosta Drive, Ocho Rios

Description: Positioned in the hills above Ocho Rios, Mystic Ridge Resort offers a blend of tranquility and accessibility. Guests can enjoy spacious suites, a swimming pool with a waterfall, and stunning panoramic views.

6. Kaz Kreol Beach Lodge

Address: Main Street, Ocho Rios

Description: A budget-friendly option, Kaz Kreol Beach Lodge provides a charming and cozy atmosphere. Located right on the beach, it's an excellent choice for those who want to be in the heart of the action without breaking the bank.

7. Shaw Park Beach Hotel & Spa

Address: Cutlass Bay, Ocho Rios

Description: Situated on a private beach, Shaw Park Beach Hotel & Spa offers a mix of elegance and Caribbean flair. With its spa, water sports, and proximity to local attractions, it caters to both relaxation seekers and adventure enthusiasts.

8. Hermosa Cove – Jamaica's Villa Hotel

Address: Pineapple, Ocho Rios

Description: Providing a unique experience, Hermosa Cove combines the privacy of villa living with the amenities of a luxury hotel. Each villa is individually designed, surrounded by lush gardens and just steps away from the Caribbean Sea.

9. Fisherman's Point Resort

Address: Turtle River Road, Ocho Rios

Description: Ideally located in the heart of Ocho Rios, Fisherman's Point Resort offers spacious apartments with kitchenettes. The property features a pool overlooking the ocean and is within walking distance of popular attractions.

10. Casa de Shalom

Address: Pineapple, Ocho Rios

Description: A boutique guesthouse, Casa de Shalom provides an intimate and personalized experience. With its charming décor, friendly staff, and proximity to Ocho Rios's main attractions, it's a hidden gem for those seeking a cozy retreat.

These resorts and hotels in Ocho Rios cater to a diverse range of preferences and budgets, ensuring that every traveler can find their perfect oasis in this Caribbean paradise. Before planning your stay, consider the unique offerings of each establishment and choose the one that aligns with your vacation goals. Whether you're looking for a romantic escape, a family-friendly resort, or a budget-conscious option, Ocho Rios has the ideal accommodation for you.

Exploring Budget-Friendly Accommodation: Hostels in Ocho Rios

When it comes to exploring Jamaica on a budget, Ocho Rios offers a plethora of options, and hostels are an excellent choice for the cost-conscious traveler. This guide will take you through some of the top hostels in Ocho Rios, providing details on facilities, atmosphere, and addresses to help you plan your stay.

1. **Reggae Hostel Ocho Rios**

Address: 22 James Avenue, Ocho Rios, Jamaica

Overview: A vibrant hostel situated in the heart of Ocho Rios, Reggae Hostel is known for its lively atmosphere and social events. With both dormitory-style and private rooms, this hostel caters to a diverse range of travelers. The communal areas are adorned with reggae-inspired décor, creating a laid-back ambiance perfect for making new friends.

2. **Sunrise Hostel**

Address: 56 Main Street, Ocho Rios, Jamaica

Overview: Sunrise Hostel is a charming budget accommodation option located close to the town center. The hostel offers clean and comfortable dormitory-style rooms with shared facilities. Guests can enjoy a communal kitchen and lounge area, making it a great choice for those who prefer a more homey atmosphere.

3. **Ocean View Hostel**

Address: 8 Ocean View Drive, Ocho Rios, Jamaica

Overview: As the name suggests, Ocean View Hostel provides stunning views of the Caribbean Sea. This hostel is perched on a hill, offering a tranquil environment away from the hustle and bustle. The spacious dormitories and outdoor terrace make it an ideal choice for travelers seeking a relaxed and scenic setting.

4. **Mystic Mountain Hostel**

Address: 45 Mystic Lane, Ocho Rios, Jamaica

Overview: Nestled near the famous Mystic Mountain attraction, this hostel combines affordability with a unique location. The hostel is surrounded by lush greenery, providing a natural and serene atmosphere. The friendly staff and communal BBQ area contribute to a warm and inviting environment.

5. Jamaican Vibes Hostel

Address: 10 Mango Street, Ocho Rios, Jamaica

Overview: Jamaican Vibes Hostel lives up to its name, offering guests an authentic Jamaican experience. With colorful décor and a focus on local culture, this hostel provides a lively and spirited atmosphere. The communal spaces are designed for socializing, making it a fantastic choice for solo travelers looking to connect with others.

6. Island Breeze Hostel

Address: 30 Palm Tree Avenue, Ocho Rios, Jamaica

Overview: Located just a short walk from the beach, Island Breeze Hostel provides a convenient and budget-friendly accommodation option. The hostel features a mix of dormitory and private rooms, ensuring a comfortable stay for all guests. The friendly staff is always ready to assist with travel tips and local recommendations.

7. Dunn's River Hostel

Address: 15 Dunn's River Road, Ocho Rios, Jamaica

Overview: Situated in close proximity to the iconic Dunn's River Falls, this hostel is a haven for nature enthusiasts. The hostel's communal terrace offers breathtaking views of the waterfall, creating a unique and picturesque setting. The simple yet cozy rooms make Dunn's River Hostel a charming choice for budget travelers.

Choosing a hostel in Ocho Rios opens up opportunities to experience the vibrant culture of Jamaica while keeping your travel expenses in check. Each of these hostels offers a unique atmosphere, ensuring that there's a budget-friendly option for every type of traveler. Before embarking on your Jamaican adventure, consider the location, facilities, and overall vibe of these hostels to find the perfect fit for your stay. Enjoy your time in Ocho Rios!

Shopping in Ocho Rios: A Retail Paradise in Jamaica

Whether you're a souvenir collector, a fashion enthusiast, or someone in search of local crafts, Ocho Rios offers a diverse array of shopping opportunities. In this guide, we'll explore the best

shopping destinations in Ocho Rios, providing you with a comprehensive overview and even including addresses to help you navigate this retail paradise.

1. **Island Village Shopping Centre**

Address: Island Village, Turtle River Road, Ocho Rios, Jamaica

Situated in the heart of Ocho Rios, the Island Village Shopping Centre is a popular destination for both locals and tourists. This open-air shopping complex combines retail therapy with entertainment, featuring a variety of shops, restaurants, and even a movie theater. Here, you can find everything from duty-free items and designer clothing to unique Jamaican crafts and souvenirs. Take a leisurely stroll through the village, enjoy live music, and immerse yourself in the vibrant atmosphere.

2. **Taj Mahal Shopping Center**

Address: 8 Main St, Ocho Rios, Jamaica

For those looking for a more traditional Jamaican shopping experience, the Taj Mahal Shopping Center is a must-visit. Located on Main Street, this bustling market offers a kaleidoscope of colors and an array of stalls selling local handicrafts, artwork, spices, and more. Bargaining is a common practice here, so don't hesitate to engage with the friendly vendors and secure some unique treasures to take home.

3. **Sonis Plaza**

Address: 1 DaCosta Dr, Ocho Rios, Jamaica

Sonis Plaza is a contemporary shopping center that caters to those seeking international brands and upscale products. From high-end fashion stores to jewelry boutiques, Sonis Plaza provides a luxurious shopping experience. After indulging in some retail therapy, take a break at one of the plaza's cafes or restaurants for a taste of Jamaican and international cuisine.

4. Craft Market Ocho Rios

Address: 17 DaCosta Dr, Ocho Rios, Jamaica

For an authentic Jamaican shopping adventure, head to the Craft Market in Ocho Rios. Located near the cruise ship terminal, this market is a treasure trove of handmade crafts, wood carvings,

and vibrant textiles. Engage with local artisans, learn about their craft, and take home one-of-a-kind pieces that reflect the rich culture of Jamaica.

5. Ocho Rios Jerk Centre

Address: 103 Main St, Ocho Rios, Jamaica

No visit to Jamaica is complete without savoring the island's famous jerk cuisine. The Ocho Rios Jerk Centre not only offers mouthwatering jerk dishes but also provides an opportunity for some culinary shopping. Stock up on authentic Jamaican jerk seasonings, sauces, and spices to recreate the island's flavors in your own kitchen.

6. Pineapple Craft Market

Address: 22 Main St, Ocho Rios, Jamaica

If you have a penchant for all things pineapple, the Pineapple Craft Market is the place to be. This market specializes in pineapple-themed souvenirs, gifts, and local products. From pineapple-shaped trinkets to delicious pineapple jams, you'll find a plethora of items to celebrate this tropical fruit.

7. Times Square Mall

Address: Main St, Ocho Rios, Jamaica

Conveniently located on Main Street, Times Square Mall is a modern shopping complex that caters to diverse tastes. Whether you're looking for fashion, electronics, or local artwork, the mall has a range of stores to explore. It's a great spot to escape the sun for a while and indulge in some air-conditioned shopping.

   8. **Casa de Oro**

Address: 22 Main St, Ocho Rios, Jamaica

If you're in the market for duty-free jewelry and luxury watches, Casa de Oro is the place to visit. Located on Main Street, this upscale store offers a curated selection of high-quality jewelry, including pieces featuring Jamaica's famous Blue Mountain Coffee gems. The knowledgeable staff can assist you in finding the perfect piece to commemorate your visit.

Ocho Rios, with its diverse shopping options, caters to every type of shopper. Whether you're seeking traditional Jamaican crafts, international brands, or unique culinary delights, the town's shopping scene has something for everyone. Remember to explore beyond the mainstream stores, engage with local vendors, and immerse yourself in the vibrant culture that makes shopping in Ocho Rios a memorable experience. Happy shopping!

Exploring Ocho Rios: Beaches and Water Activities

Ocho Rios is renowned for its stunning beaches and a plethora of water activities that cater to both thrill-seekers and those seeking a more relaxed seaside experience. Here's a detailed exploration of the beaches and water adventures that await you in Ocho Rios.

   1. **Dunn's River Falls**

Address: Ocho Rios, St. Ann, Jamaica

Dunn's River Falls is an iconic natural attraction that blends adventure with breathtaking beauty. The cascading waterfalls provide a unique opportunity for visitors to climb the terraced steps, guided by experienced locals. The cool, crystal-clear water offers a refreshing escape, and the surrounding lush greenery enhances the scenic beauty.

   2. **Mystic Mountain**

Address: Rainforest Adventures, Ocho Rios, Jamaica

Mystic Mountain is not just about beaches; it's an adventure park that offers a range of water-based activities. The Bobsled Jamaica ride takes you through the rainforest, and the Rainforest Zip Line offers an adrenaline-pumping experience with panoramic views of Ocho Rios. The park also features an infinity-edge pool, allowing you to relax while enjoying the scenery.

3. Mahogany Beach

Address: Mahogany Beach, Ocho Rios, Jamaica

For a more laid-back beach experience, Mahogany Beach is an excellent choice. It boasts soft golden sand and calm turquoise waters. Visitors can indulge in various water activities such as

snorkeling, kayaking, and paddleboarding. The beach is lined with vibrant beach bars and local vendors, providing an authentic Jamaican atmosphere.

4. Turtle River Falls and Gardens

Address: 3 Crane Road, Ocho Rios, Jamaica

While not a traditional beach, Turtle River Falls and Gardens offer a unique water-centric experience. Explore the lush gardens and discover hidden waterfalls and pools. The serene environment is perfect for a leisurely stroll, and you can even take a dip in the natural springs for a refreshing break.

5. Ocho Rios Bay Beach

Address: Ocho Rios Bay Beach, Ocho Rios, Jamaica

Located near the town center, Ocho Rios Bay Beach is a public beach with a lively atmosphere. The shallow, clear waters make it ideal for swimming and snorkeling. The beach is also equipped with facilities like changing rooms and local eateries, making it convenient for a full day of seaside relaxation.

6. Island Gully Falls (Blue Hole)

Address: Island Gully Falls, Ocho Rios, Jamaica

For a more off-the-beaten-path adventure, head to Island Gully Falls, commonly known as the Blue Hole. This secluded spot features stunning turquoise pools surrounded by lush greenery.

Dive into the refreshing waters from various heights, or simply enjoy the natural beauty of this hidden gem.

7. **Reggae Beach**

Address: Reggae Beach, Ocho Rios, Jamaica

Reggae Beach offers a perfect blend of entertainment and relaxation. With its soft sand and clear waters, it's an ideal spot for swimming and sunbathing. The beach often hosts live music events, adding a touch of Jamaica's vibrant culture to your seaside experience.

SECTION 4: ACTIVITIES AND EXCURSIONS

Hiking and Nature Trails in Jamaica: A Journey Through Paradise

Jamaica, known for its sun-kissed beaches and vibrant culture, also offers a hidden gem for nature enthusiasts and adventure seekers – its diverse and breathtaking hiking trails. From lush rainforests to cascading waterfalls, the island is a paradise for those who yearn to explore the great outdoors. Here, we delve into some of the most captivating hiking and nature trails in Jamaica.

1. **Blue Mountains National Park**

Address: Blue Mountains, Jamaica

The Blue Mountains, towering over eastern Jamaica, are home to some of the island's most challenging yet rewarding hiking trails. The Blue Mountains National Park, a UNESCO World Heritage Site, boasts an extensive network of trails that cater to various skill levels. The famous Blue Mountain Peak Trail takes hikers to the island's highest point, offering breathtaking panoramic views of the surrounding landscape.

As you ascend through mist-shrouded forests, you'll encounter unique flora and fauna found only in these mountains. Be prepared for a cool climate and occasional rain showers, making the journey even more enchanting.

2. Dunn's River Falls Trail

Address: Ocho Rios, Jamaica

Dunn's River Falls, one of Jamaica's most iconic natural attractions, offers not just a sight to behold but also an exhilarating hike. The trail allows visitors to climb the terraced limestone steps of the waterfall, guided by experienced locals.

Wading through the crystal-clear waters and navigating the naturally formed rock steps, you'll experience a refreshing and challenging adventure. The trail is suitable for all skill levels, making it a must-visit for families and solo adventurers alike.

3. Mayfield Falls

Address: Glenbrook, Westmoreland, Jamaica

Nestled in the scenic hills of Westmoreland, Mayfield Falls is a hidden gem for nature lovers. The trail to Mayfield Falls winds through bamboo groves, tropical gardens, and riverbeds. Visitors can take a guided tour along the trail, exploring the twenty-one natural pools and waterfalls that make up Mayfield Falls.

What sets Mayfield Falls apart is the interactive experience – hikers can swim, climb, and even get a natural massage under the cascading water. It's a serene escape into the heart of Jamaica's lush interior.

4. Cockpit Country

Address: Trelawny, Jamaica

For a unique and off-the-beaten-path hiking experience, venture into the rugged terrain of Cockpit Country. This limestone plateau is marked by its distinctive mogote hills and lush valleys. The Cockpit Country Trail takes hikers through dense forests, revealing a rich biodiversity that includes rare and endemic species.

As you navigate the trails, keep an eye out for the indigenous flora and fauna, including the vibrant Jamaican swallowtail butterfly. The Cockpit Country is a haven for birdwatchers and those seeking solitude in nature's embrace.

5. Reach Falls

Address: Manchioneal, Portland, Jamaica

Located in the parish of Portland, Reach Falls is a lesser-known but equally enchanting destination for hikers. The trail leading to Reach Falls winds through bamboo forests and alongside the Swift River. The reward at the end is a stunning waterfall cascading into a series of azure pools.

Hikers can explore the hidden caves behind the waterfall and take a refreshing dip in the natural pools. Reach Falls is a true testament to Jamaica's untouched beauty and a haven for those seeking a tranquil escape.

Tips for Hiking in Jamaica

Guided Tours: While some trails can be explored independently, considering a guided tour can enhance your experience by providing insights into the local flora, fauna, and cultural significance.

Proper Gear: Wear comfortable and sturdy hiking shoes, carry a water bottle, and pack essentials like sunscreen and insect repellent. The tropical climate can be unpredictable, so a light rain jacket is advisable.

Respect the Environment: Preserve Jamaica's natural beauty by adhering to Leave No Trace principles. Stay on designated trails, refrain from littering, and respect wildlife.

Jamaica's hiking and nature trails offer a diverse range of experiences, from challenging mountain treks to serene river walks. Whichever trail you choose, you're sure to be captivated by the island's natural wonders and the warm hospitality of its people. Lace up your hiking boots and embark on a journey through Jamaica's paradise of trails!

Reggae Music and Dance in Jamaica

Jamaica, a vibrant island nation in the Caribbean, is not only renowned for its stunning beaches and lush landscapes but also for its globally influential music and dance culture, with reggae reigning supreme. Rooted in the island's history and the struggles of its people, reggae has evolved into a powerful form of expression, reflecting the spirit and identity of Jamaica.

Historical Roots:

Reggae emerged in the late 1960s, drawing inspiration from various musical genres such as mento, ska, and rocksteady. It is deeply connected to the socio-political landscape of Jamaica, with lyrics often addressing issues of social justice, inequality, and resistance. The pulsating rhythms of reggae are a testament to the resilience and creativity of the Jamaican people.

Musical Elements:

Characterized by a distinctive offbeat rhythm, reggae features a prominent use of the guitar, bass, and drums. The heartbeat of reggae is the iconic "one drop" rhythm, where emphasis is placed on the third beat of the bar. This rhythmic pattern, coupled with soulful melodies and meaningful lyrics, creates a unique and powerful musical experience.

Bob Marley and the Wailers:

No exploration of reggae would be complete without mentioning the legendary Bob Marley. His impact on the genre and its global recognition cannot be overstated. Marley's socially conscious lyrics, coupled with his soulful voice, made him an international symbol of reggae music. The Wailers, the band he co-founded, played a pivotal role in shaping the reggae sound and spreading its message worldwide.

Dancehall Influence:

In addition to reggae, Jamaica is also home to the lively dancehall genre. Emerging in the late 1970s, dancehall music is characterized by its faster tempo and electronic beats. Dancehall has its roots in reggae but has evolved into a genre with its own distinct sound and dance culture. The energetic and expressive dance moves associated with dancehall are an integral part of Jamaican social life and entertainment.

Dance as Expression:

Dance plays a crucial role in the reggae and dancehall culture. It is a form of expression that goes beyond mere entertainment; it is a way of communicating emotions, stories, and cultural identity. Traditional Jamaican dances, such as the ska, rocksteady, and the more contemporary dancehall moves, are a vibrant part of the island's cultural fabric.

Social and Political Commentary:

Reggae, in particular, has been a powerful vehicle for social and political commentary. From Bob Marley's "Redemption Song" to Peter Tosh's "Equal Rights," reggae artists have used their music to advocate for change and challenge injustice. The genre's ability to address pressing issues while maintaining a rhythm that captivates audiences has contributed to its enduring popularity.

Global Impact:

Reggae's influence has transcended Jamaican borders, making it a global phenomenon. The genre has inspired musicians across the world and has been incorporated into various musical styles. Reggae festivals, both in Jamaica and internationally, celebrate the genre's rich heritage, attracting fans from diverse backgrounds.

Cultural Festivals:

Jamaica hosts numerous cultural festivals that celebrate reggae music and dance. The Reggae Sumfest, held annually in Montego Bay, is one of the largest reggae festivals globally, featuring performances by local and international artists. These festivals not only showcase the musical talent but also provide a platform for the expression of Jamaican identity and culture.

Legacy and Future:

The legacy of reggae in Jamaica is deeply ingrained in the national psyche. It continues to evolve, with contemporary artists infusing new elements while staying true to its roots.

Reggae's enduring popularity speaks to its ability to resonate with people on a profound level, connecting them to the history, struggles, and triumphs of the Jamaican people.

Reggae music and dance are integral components of Jamaica's cultural identity. Beyond the infectious rhythms and captivating dance moves, they serve as powerful forms of expression, conveying the history, struggles, and aspirations of the Jamaican people. As reggae continues to inspire and influence generations globally, it remains a beacon of cultural pride for Jamaica, a small island with a big musical heart.

Local Festivals and Events in Jamaica

Jamaica, with its vibrant culture and lively spirit, hosts a plethora of festivals and events throughout the year. These celebrations showcase the island's rich heritage, artistic talents, and the warmth of its people. While the exact dates may vary, here are some of the most anticipated festivals and events that you might want to consider when planning your visit to Jamaica.

1. **Reggae Sumfest**

Location: Montego Bay

Reggae Sumfest is Jamaica's premier reggae music festival, drawing music enthusiasts from around the world. This annual event typically takes place in July and features performances by both local and international reggae artists. From pulsating rhythms to soulful melodies, Reggae Sumfest is a celebration of Jamaica's musical prowess.

2. **Jamaica Carnival**

Location: Kingston

Embracing the vibrant spirit of Caribbean carnival culture, Jamaica Carnival is a lively and colorful event that usually takes place in April. Participants don elaborate costumes, dance to infectious rhythms, and celebrate the island's unity through music and dance. The parade through the streets of Kingston is a highlight, showcasing the creativity and energy of the participants.

3. **Bob Marley Week**

Location: Various

Celebrated around the world, Bob Marley Week in Jamaica is a special time to honor the legendary reggae icon. Usually held in early February, this week features concerts, tribute events, and gatherings at the Bob Marley Museum in Kingston. It's a time when fans and music lovers come together to pay homage to the enduring legacy of the "King of Reggae."

4. *Jamaica Independence Celebrations*

Location: Nationwide

Jamaica gained independence on August 6, and the entire nation comes alive with festivities to commemorate this historic event. From parades and concerts to cultural exhibitions, the Independence Celebrations in early August reflect the pride Jamaicans have in their history and the vibrant diversity of their culture.

5. *Jamaica Film Festival*

Location: Kingston

Film enthusiasts and industry professionals gather in Kingston for the Jamaica Film Festival, typically held in July. This event showcases the best of Jamaican and Caribbean cinema, providing a platform for filmmakers to present their work and fostering a deeper appreciation for the region's storytelling through film.

6. *Portland Jerk Festival*

Location: Portland

For food lovers, the Portland Jerk Festival is a must-attend event. Celebrating Jamaica's renowned jerk cuisine, this festival usually takes place in July. Visitors can savor a variety of jerk dishes, enjoy live music, and experience the unique flavors that make Jamaican cuisine a culinary delight.

7. *Accompong Maroon Festival*

Location: Accompong

The Accompong Maroon Festival is a cultural extravaganza held in January to celebrate the anniversary of the signing of the peace treaty between the Maroons and the British in 1739. This event, taking place in the Maroon community of Accompong, features traditional music, dance, and rituals that honor the resilience and heritage of the Maroon people.

8. Ocho Rios Jazz Festival

Location: Ocho Rios

Jazz enthusiasts flock to Ocho Rios for the annual Ocho Rios Jazz Festival, a week-long celebration of smooth melodies and soulful tunes. The festival, often held in June, showcases a mix of local and international jazz artists, creating a magical atmosphere along the picturesque northern coast of Jamaica.

These festivals and events offer a glimpse into the heart and soul of Jamaica, showcasing the island's cultural richness and creative spirit. Keep an eye on official event calendars for specific dates and plan your visit to coincide with these lively celebrations for an unforgettable Jamaican experience.

SECTION 5: CUISINE

Jamaican Dishes to Try

Jamaican cuisine is a delightful fusion of flavors, influenced by the island's rich history and cultural diversity. From savory stews to spicy jerked meats, here are some must-try dishes that will tantalize your taste buds during your visit to Jamaica.

1. Jerk Chicken

Description: Jerk chicken is a Jamaican classic known for its bold and spicy flavor. The chicken is marinated in a mixture of Scotch bonnet peppers, thyme, scallions, and various spices before being slow-cooked over pimento wood. The result is tender, smoky, and incredibly flavorful chicken.

Availability: Found in local jerk centers, street food stalls, and many traditional Jamaican restaurants.

2. *Ackee and Saltfish*

Description: Considered the national dish of Jamaica, ackee and saltfish is a savory and satisfying combination. Ackee, a fruit native to West Africa, is sautéed with salted codfish, onions, tomatoes, and spices. It's often served with fried dumplings or boiled green bananas.

Availability: Available in most Jamaican restaurants, particularly those specializing in traditional cuisine.

3. *Curried Goat*

Description: A flavorful curry made with tender goat meat, potatoes, and a medley of spices. This dish reflects the Indian influence on Jamaican cuisine and is often served with rice and peas.

Availability: Common in local eateries, especially those focusing on traditional Jamaican fare.

4. *Escovitch Fish*

Description: This dish features fried fish topped with a spicy and tangy pickled vegetable medley, including carrots, onions, and Scotch bonnet peppers. It's a delightful combination of crispy and zesty flavors.

Availability: Found in coastal areas, particularly at seafood restaurants and local fish markets.

5. *Bammy*

Description: Bammy is a flatbread made from cassava that is often served with fish dishes. It has a unique texture and is gluten-free, making it a staple in Jamaican cuisine.

Availability: Widely available in restaurants that serve traditional Jamaican meals.

6. *Pepper Pot Soup*

Description: A hearty soup made with callaloo (amaranth leaves), okra, peppered beef, and various other vegetables. It's a comforting and nutritious choice, often enjoyed as a main course.

Availability: Featured on the menu in many local soup kitchens and traditional eateries.

7. *Jamaican Patty*

Description: A flaky pastry filled with seasoned meat, such as beef, chicken, or vegetable. Jamaican patties are a popular street food snack and can be enjoyed on the go.

Availability: Found in bakeries, street food stalls, and local markets across the island.

8. *Rice and Peas*

Description: A staple side dish in Jamaican cuisine, rice and peas feature rice cooked with coconut milk, kidney beans, thyme, and Scotch bonnet pepper. It's often served alongside jerk chicken or curried dishes.

Availability: Included as a side dish in many Jamaican restaurants.

9. *Bamboo Chicken*

Description: Chicken seasoned with a blend of herbs and spices, then wrapped in bamboo leaves and slow-cooked over an open flame. The bamboo imparts a unique smoky flavor to the chicken.

Availability: Common at local festivals and events celebrating Jamaican cuisine.

10. *Toto*

Description: A traditional Jamaican coconut cake made with grated coconut, flour, sugar, and spices. Toto is a sweet and moist dessert often enjoyed with a cup of Jamaican Blue Mountain coffee.

Availability: Featured in bakeries and dessert shops across the island.

Exploring Jamaican Cuisine

While these descriptions provide a taste of Jamaican culinary delights, the best way to truly experience the island's food culture is to venture into local markets, street food stalls, and traditional eateries. Embrace the vibrant flavors, engage with local chefs, and savor the authenticity of Jamaican cuisine during your culinary journey through this Caribbean gem.

A Gastronomic Journey through Jamaican Street Food Delights

In this culinary exploration, we'll delve into the diverse and flavorful world of Jamaican street food, providing insights into the unique dishes, the artisans behind them, and where you can savor these delights.

1. **Jerk Chicken at Scotchies**

Location: Scotchies Jerk Center, Ocho Rios

Nestled in the heart of Ocho Rios, Scotchies is a legendary spot for jerk chicken enthusiasts. The air is filled with the aromatic blend of pimento wood smoke as skilled chefs grill chicken to

perfection. The succulent, smoky flavor of Scotchies' jerk chicken is a culinary experience not to be missed.

2. **Peppered Shrimp on Middle Quarters Road**

Location: Middle Quarters Road, Middle Quarters

Middle Quarters is renowned for its spicy and succulent peppered shrimp. Vendors line the road, skillfully preparing this delicacy with a secret blend of spices. Join the locals in the roadside feast, savoring the heat and flavor of freshly caught shrimp.

3. **Doubles Delight in Downtown Kingston**

Location: Downtown Kingston

Venture into the bustling streets of downtown Kingston to discover the beloved Trinidadian import – Doubles. A fusion of Indian and Caribbean flavors, Doubles are a delightful street snack featuring curried chickpeas sandwiched between two fluffy bara (fried flatbreads). Explore the diverse stalls offering this savory treat.

4. Mannish Water on Duke Street

Location: Duke Street, Kingston

For the adventurous foodie, Mannish Water is a must-try traditional Jamaican soup made from goat's head, tripe, and various spices. Seek out the vibrant stalls on Duke Street in Kingston to sample this hearty and flavorsome soup, a favorite among locals.

5. Escovitch Fish at Hellshire Beach

Location: Hellshire Beach, Portmore

Indulge in the freshest catch of the day at Hellshire Beach, where vendors serve up Escovitch Fish, a dish featuring fried fish topped with a spicy vinegar-based dressing. The seaside setting adds to the charm, creating a perfect culinary experience by the waves.

6. Bammy Delicacies in Falmouth

Location: Falmouth, Trelawny

Explore the historic town of Falmouth to discover the unique street food scene. Bammy, a flatbread made from cassava, takes center stage here. Try it with fried fish or Ackee and Saltfish for an authentic taste of Jamaican culinary tradition.

7. Patty Paradise on Orange Street

Location: Orange Street, Kingston

Orange Street in Kingston is a patty lover's paradise. These flaky pastry pockets filled with spicy and savory fillings, such as jerk chicken or curried beef, are a Jamaican street food staple. Sample patties from different vendors to discover your favorite.

8. Sugar Cane Euphoria in St. Elizabeth

Location: Bamboo Avenue, St. Elizabeth

Satisfy your sweet tooth with the natural sweetness of sugar cane. Visit Bamboo Avenue in St. Elizabeth, where vendors skillfully peel and cut sugar cane for a refreshing and healthy street snack. It's a delightful way to experience the island's natural flavors.

Jamaican street food is a celebration of the island's rich culinary tapestry, offering a diverse and flavorful array of dishes. From the fiery jerk chicken at Scotchies to the sweet crunch of sugar cane along Bamboo Avenue, each street food experience is a journey into Jamaica's cultural and gastronomic heritage. As you explore the vibrant streets and markets, let the enticing aromas and bold flavors guide you through this unforgettable culinary adventure. So, hit the streets, follow your nose, and savor the authentic tastes of Jamaica's street food scene.

Fine Dining Experiences in Jamaica

Jamaica, known for its vibrant culture and breathtaking landscapes, also offers a diverse and exquisite culinary scene. While the island is famous for its jerk chicken and spicy curries, it's also home to a range of upscale dining establishments that cater to those seeking a sophisticated and refined culinary experience. Here are some fine dining restaurants in Jamaica that promise not only delectable cuisine but also an unforgettable ambiance.

1. **The Sugar Mill Restaurant**

Situated in the Half Moon Resort in Montego Bay, The Sugar Mill Restaurant is a culinary gem that combines modern Jamaican flavors with international influences. Set in an 18th-century plantation house, the restaurant exudes elegance and charm. Guests can savor dishes like grilled lobster tail with mango salsa or jerk-spiced lamb, all while surrounded by lush tropical gardens.

2. **Norma's at the Marina**

Located in Kingston at the Morgan's Harbour Hotel, Norma's at the Marina is a culinary haven founded by the renowned chef Norma Shirley. The restaurant boasts a picturesque setting overlooking the Kingston Harbor. The menu features a fusion of Caribbean and international cuisines, with signature dishes like curried coconut shrimp and ackee spring rolls.

3. The Cliff Restaurant

Perched on the cliffs of Negril's West End, The Cliff Restaurant offers a panoramic ocean view and an intimate dining experience. Known for its seafood and Jamaican fusion cuisine, this restaurant has an extensive wine list to complement its delectable dishes. The ambiance, with candlelit tables and the sound of the waves crashing below, creates a romantic and magical atmosphere.

4. Blue Window Restaurant

Situated in the Jamaica Pegasus Hotel in Kingston, the Blue Window Restaurant is a fine dining establishment that serves a mix of Jamaican and international dishes. The elegant décor and attentive service make it a popular choice for both locals and visitors. From traditional Jamaican breakfasts to gourmet dinners, the menu caters to a variety of tastes.

5. Evita's Italian Restaurant

Nestled in the hills of Ocho Rios, Evita's Italian Restaurant offers a departure from traditional Jamaican cuisine with its focus on authentic Italian dishes. The restaurant is set in a historic

house with a beautiful garden, providing a romantic and charming atmosphere. Guests can enjoy classic Italian pasta dishes, seafood, and a selection of fine wines.

6. Mystic India

For those seeking a break from Jamaican and international flavors, Mystic India in Montego Bay provides an exceptional Indian dining experience. The restaurant, known for its authentic Indian cuisine, offers a diverse menu featuring flavorful curries, tandoori specialties, and traditional Indian desserts. The vibrant and colorful setting adds to the overall dining experience.

7. Round Hill Dining

Situated in the Round Hill Hotel and Villas in Montego Bay, Round Hill Dining offers an elegant and refined dining experience. With a focus on fresh, locally sourced ingredients, the menu showcases a blend of international and Caribbean flavors. Guests can enjoy their meals in a sophisticated setting with stunning views of the Caribbean Sea.

Jamaica's fine dining scene is a testament to the island's ability to blend its rich culinary heritage with global influences. Whether you're a visitor or a local looking for a special night out, these fine dining establishments in Jamaica promise an unforgettable experience that goes beyond just satisfying your taste buds.

Beverage Specialties in Jamaica

When it comes to beverages in Jamaica, the island offers a vibrant and diverse array of drinks that reflect its rich cultural heritage. From traditional favorites to modern twists, exploring Jamaican beverages is a delightful journey for the taste buds.

1. **Blue Mountain Coffee**

Description: Renowned as one of the world's best coffees, Blue Mountain Coffee is grown in the cool, misty hills of the Blue Mountains. The unique climate and rich soil contribute to its exceptional flavor.

Address: Visit the Blue Mountains Coffee Estate, Mavis Bank, Kingston.

2. **Jamaican Rum Punch**

Description: A quintessential Jamaican cocktail, Rum Punch combines the bold flavors of Jamaican rum with tropical fruit juices. It's a refreshing drink that captures the essence of the Caribbean.

Address: Enjoy a classic Rum Punch at Rick's Café, West End Road, Negril.

3. **Sorrel Drink**

Description: A popular festive drink, Sorrel is made from the petals of the sorrel plant, ginger, and spices. It's often enjoyed during Christmas and other special occasions.

Address: Sample authentic Sorrel at Devon House I-Scream, 26 Hope Road, Kingston.

4. Jamaican Ginger Beer

Description: This non-alcoholic beverage packs a punch with its intense ginger flavor. It's a favorite among locals for its refreshing and spicy kick.

Address: Find Jamaican Ginger Beer at local markets and street vendors throughout the island.

5. Jelly Coconut Water

Description: Fresh coconut water straight from a young green coconut is a popular and healthy choice to stay hydrated in the Jamaican heat. The jelly-like flesh inside adds a unique texture.

Address: Purchase Jelly Coconut from street vendors along popular beaches like Doctor's Cave Beach, Montego Bay.

6. Peanut Punch

Description: A nutritious and delicious beverage, Peanut Punch combines peanuts, milk, and a hint of nutmeg. It's a fulfilling drink often consumed for breakfast or as an energy booster.

Address: Try Peanut Punch at local cafes such as Café Blue, Sovereign Centre, Kingston.

7. Jamaican Craft Beer

Description: The craft beer scene is booming in Jamaica, with breweries producing unique flavors inspired by local ingredients. From fruity ales to robust stouts, there's something for every beer enthusiast.

Address: Visit the Red Stripe Brewery, 214 Spanish Town Road, Kingston, for a tour and tasting session.

8. Soursop Juice

Description: Made from the soursop fruit, this sweet and tangy juice is not only delicious but also believed to have health benefits. It's a tropical treat worth trying.

Address: Find Soursop Juice at local fruit stalls in popular markets like Coronation Market, Kingston.

9. Pepper Pot Soup

Description: While not a beverage in the traditional sense, Pepper Pot Soup, made with callaloo, okra, and peppered beef, is a hearty and flavorful soup enjoyed throughout Jamaica.

Address: Taste authentic Pepper Pot Soup at local roadside stalls in rural areas.

10. Bammy Colada

Description: A Jamaican twist on the classic piña colada, the Bammy Colada incorporates bammy, a flatbread made from cassava, into the mix. It's a unique and tasty cocktail.

Address: Experience the Bammy Colada at resorts like Sandals Ochi Beach Resort, Main Street, Ocho Rios.

Jamaica's beverage scene is as diverse as its culture, offering a taste of the island's history and traditions in every sip. Whether you're a coffee connoisseur, a rum enthusiast, or simply looking to quench your thirst with tropical delights, Jamaica has something special for every palate.

PRATICIAL TIPS

The Rich Tapestry of Jamaican Phrases: A Linguistic Journey

Jamaica, a land known for its warm sun, reggae rhythms, and lush landscapes, is equally renowned for its colorful and distinctive language. The Jamaican patois, a creole language that developed from a blend of African, European, and indigenous influences, is a treasure trove of expressions that reflect the island's history, culture, and vibrant spirit. In this exploration, we delve into 3000 words on common phrases in Jamaica, unraveling the linguistic tapestry that makes the Jamaican language truly unique.

1. Greetings and Salutations

In Jamaica, greetings are more than just polite exchanges; they are an art form. The ubiquitous "Wah gwaan?" meaning "What's going on?" or "How are you?" is the go-to greeting, reflecting the laid-back and friendly nature of Jamaican culture. Responding with "Mi deh yah" signals that all is well, and you're present in the moment.

The warmth extends to farewell expressions like "Mi deh yah, nuh worry yuhself," reassuring that you'll be around, so there's no need to worry.

2. Everyday Expressions

Jamaicans infuse their everyday conversations with lively expressions that add flavor to communication. "Likkle more" doesn't mean a small quantity but is a farewell, promising to meet again soon. "Mi deh yah man" signifies a sense of contentment and presence.

When someone exclaims "Yow!" or "Wah di bloodclaat?" it's an expression of surprise or disbelief, and it reflects the candid and expressive nature of Jamaican speech.

3. Terms of Endearment

Jamaicans are known for their warmth and affectionate mannerisms. "Mi love" doesn't necessarily imply romantic love; it's a term of endearment used among friends and family. "Mi deh yah pon a love mission" suggests spreading positive vibes and love wherever you go.

Addressing someone as "Breda" or "Sista" regardless of blood relations indicates a strong sense of camaraderie and community.

4. Food and Culinary Delights

Jamaican cuisine is a symphony of flavors, and the language associated with it is equally delightful. "Nyam" means to eat with gusto, and when someone says "Mi belly full," it's a testament to a satisfying meal. "Likkle more food" expresses anticipation for the next delicious bite.

If someone offers you "Likkle piece a di pot," they are extending a warm invitation to share in the culinary delights of their home.

5. Celebrations and Praise

Jamaicans know how to celebrate, and their expressions of joy are infectious. "Big up" is a term of praise, acknowledgment, and respect. "Mi rate yuh" means that you are highly regarded or respected in someone's eyes.

When festivities are in full swing, you might hear "Di vibes tun up," signifying that the energy and excitement have reached a peak.

6. Expressions of Resilience

Resilience is a hallmark of Jamaican culture, and it is reflected in the language. "Wi likkle but wi tallawah" encapsulates the spirit of overcoming challenges with determination and strength. "No weh nuh betta dan yard" conveys a deep appreciation for home, no matter where in the world you may be.

In times of difficulty, the phrase "Out of many, one people" emphasizes unity and solidarity in facing adversity.

7. Spirituality and Mysticism

Jamaica's spiritual and mystical traditions influence its language, adding a layer of depth and reverence. "Irie" is not just a word; it's a state of being, representing harmony and positivity. "Mi deh pon a higher meditation" indicates a contemplative and spiritual mindset.

The phrase "Walk good" isn't just about the physical act of walking; it carries a spiritual wish for a safe and prosperous journey.

8. Music and Dance

Reggae music and dance are integral to Jamaican culture, and the language associated with them is equally rhythmic. "Buss a wine" invites you to join in a dance, expressing the freedom and joy found on the dancefloor. "Rub-a-dub" signifies a lively dancehall session filled with reggae beats and energetic moves.

When someone exclaims "Mi deh pon di riddim," it means they are in sync with the music and feeling the groove.

9. Slang and Informal Expressions

Jamaican slang adds an informal and playful dimension to the language. "Gyal" is an informal term for a girl or woman, often used with affection. "Mi deh yah pon di ends" means being present in the local neighborhood or community.

Slang terms like "Mash up" (to destroy or defeat) and "Flex" (to show off or impress) are woven into everyday conversations, giving them a dynamic and contemporary flair.

10. Time and Jamaican Timing

In Jamaica, time has its own rhythm, often referred to as "Jamaican time." "Soon come" doesn't necessarily mean imminent arrival but reflects a relaxed approach to schedules. "Mi reach" announces your arrival, often accompanied by a sense of accomplishment.

When someone says "Mi deh yah from mawnin," it doesn't necessarily mean they've been there since morning; it's a colloquial expression emphasizing the duration of their presence.

The common phrases in Jamaica are not just linguistic expressions; they are windows into the soul of a vibrant and resilient culture. Each phrase carries with it the history, warmth, and rhythmic cadence that define the Jamaican experience. So, whether you're navigating the bustling streets of Kingston or enjoying the laid-back vibes of the beach, embracing these phrases will undoubtedly enhance your journey through the heart and soul of Jamaica. Mi deh yah!

Made in the USA
Columbia, SC
31 January 2025